G000152678

LITTLE BOOK OF
CARAVANS

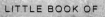

LITTLE BOOK OF

CARAVANS

First published in the UK in 2011

© G2 Entertainment Limited 2013

www.G2ent.co.uk

Printed and bound printed in the EU

ISBN 978-1-907803-42-0

Contents

Foreword

I came to it late; you like to think you've tried most things by the time you turn forty, but there you go. It was ten years ago and I was working as a presenter on BBC's Holiday programme jetting off to any country that possessed a reputable airport, a tourist office and a half decent hotel to make six-minute films extolling the region's virtues. Then one day I got the call. The Holiday show wanted to feature a 'Do-It-Yourself' family caravan break in the north of France. As I had a family, there were five of us, and I lived near France – apparently London counts as near – would I consider it? I don't think I'd ever had cause to use the word 'caravan' in all my forty years, neither had my wife and here we were

being asked to not only tow a bloody great caravan to France with a car full of kids, but holiday in it once we got there. Madness.

Despite The Caravan Club's training session, the first time you tow a caravan on an open road it is, obviously, the most nerve-racking experience known to man. Being filmed for national television while doing it is almost beyond the call of duty, but four hours in and on French soil, I was king of the wrong side of the road. Once we, eventually, pulled up to the gates of the campsite at La Bien Assise, barely six miles inland, our lives were to change forever. We thought we'd give it a go, it would be our 'one night stand' with caravanning, make our excuses and leave. Three days were spent living out of a space that seemed no bigger than our galley kitchen at home. And we absolutely loved it.

Ten years on, in a slightly bigger caravan, we still love it, so it wasn't just a fling after all. Today, with very nearly three teenage kids, when we caravan our lives are thrown together, it's as if real life is put on hold. All thoughts of conflict or disharmony within the family, the worries and potholes of life are somehow 'put on the back burner'. We get on. Madness or what?

It's safe to say, caravanning found me as I would never have found it, and I'll remain eternally grateful for that. I'll also no longer be judging a book by its cover.

Rowland Rivron, 2011

Introduction

The production and use of caravans follows a long tradition tracing its origins back to roaming tradesmen, travelling preachers and gypsy folk, and encompasses the essential transport for circus operators, fairground showmen and their families.

It was not until the 1880s that an enthusiastic Scotsman, Dr W. Gordon Stables, chose to holiday by horse-drawn caravan – now recognised as the embryonic start of a worldwide hobby and industry.

There are those who embrace its virtues, the very purposes for which the good doctor had intended – enjoying the fresh air of the Great Outdoors in relative comfort while at the same time, not having to suffer the not so Great British weather that is the bane of many a tent-dwelling holidaymaker!

And then there are a minority of detractors. I'm afraid there's no getting away from it; the British public have a love-hate relationship with the humble leisure caravan and there are those who would perhaps, I guess, be mildly happier to see caravans banned from highways

and byways altogether!

It's not the caravan's fault of course, nor is it the fault of the vast majority of caravanners. It all seems to stem back to the austere days of the late-1940s. While Britain tried to recover from hardships resulting from the ravishes of war in Europe, poorly and hastily constructed caravans provoked the scorn of the public and press alike. A highly restrictive speed limit during a time when automobile technology had advanced tremendously only added to ill-feeling, fuelling further derisive comments from other road users.

The previously idyllic and quite innocuous pastime of leisure caravanning had earned itself, or rather been branded with an undeservedly bad name.

Thankfully, the story of the caravan is much, much more than that; a vast and

Above: A superb period shot from the mid-1920s showing a Morris Oxford hitched up to a Car Cruiser caravan, ready for the off!

Above: One of the beautifully sculpted Car Cruiser caravans of the 1930s on tour in 1937 with an Austin Six.

absorbing tale that covers the best part of two centuries, from those early tranquil days of horse-drawn innocence to the car-towed era that began just prior to World War I, from Wanderer to Willerby, Eccles to Elddis, and Pixy to Pod.

With literally hundreds of British manufacturers having been established throughout the course of caravanning history (around 400 alone in the years immediately after World War II!), it is impossible to detail every make and model ever made within the pages of this book. I

hope, however, that I have included many of the more important and influential companies that have governed the way in which this significant part of motoring heritage has developed, as well as at least touched on a few of those quirks and curiosities that go towards making this such a diverse and fascinating subject.

Incidentally, throughout the text I have used the term 'van (prefixed with an apostrophe) simply as a shortened version of the word caravan – something of a commonality among the caravanning

Left: By the mid-1960s Safari of Stroud had built a reputation for luxurious touring vans.

Below: An advertisement for *The Avondale Swift*.

fraternity!

In putting this book together, I would like to express my sincere appreciation to the following for their invaluable help with historical research and use of images:

Nikki Nichols of The Caravan Club; John Sootheran of The Caravan magazine; Simon Howard of Bailey Caravans; Mike Doherty; Matt & Becky Clay of Dub-box; Daniel Dukes; Patricia Earwicker; Richard Stark of the English Caravan Company; Lee Foster; Andy & Lesley Goplen; Mike & Sue Lanham; Dave & Beryl Lewis; Paul Nicholls; Alan Thompson; Ian & Chris Williamson; Paul & Diana Woods; and last but by no means least, from the National Motor Museum,

Beaulieu, Angela Cox of the Caravan Club Archive, the Reference Library's Patrick Collins, and Jon Day of the Motoring Picture Library – thank you all!

Steve Lanham, 2011

Made in 3 and 4 berth models, 14ft. x 6ft. 6ins. this new Caravan is Gas equipped, has Aluminium exterior and Hand-Polished Furniture.

The **AVONDALE** *Swift*

Distributed through the United British Caravan Co., Ltd. Depots.

H. FISK & SON AVONDALE WORKS DENBY DALE ROAD **WAKEFIELD**

Waggon and Horses

One might be forgiven in thinking the origins of roving by caravan began in the long tradition of Romany folk who travelled the land in search of work. It is certainly true that by the late-1800s, these families were using less tented accommodation and investing in or creating their own horse-drawn caravans. But the emergence of the timber-construction living van can be traced back at least to early 19th Century showmen who toured the country, setting up fairs, circuses and menageries of wild and exotic animals to delight villagers and townsmen in a time when the population were largely impoverished and obliged to find their own entertainment. When the

Show came to town, it was a time for relaxation, celebration, much merriment and inebriation. As rides became ever more sophisticated, the procession of vehicles arriving on the common, park or village green gradually became longer, larger packing vans required more horses to pull each one, and to provide showmen, labourers and all their families with adequate and comfortable

living, caravans became increasingly commodious and well-appointed. In line with fairground rides and stalls, living vans were decorated with ornate carved wood detailing, elaborately cut glass windows and mirrors, and flamboyant colour schemes to further enhance the spectacle on arrival.

Around 1810, when French nomadic gypsies took to roaming by horse-drawn 'vardo' (from 'vurdon', the Iranian word for 'cart'), they too displayed some extraordinary masterpieces of craftsmanship in carpentry and hand-painted embellishment. By 1850, the majority of British Romanichal tented accommodation had been replaced by the caravan, a number of manufacturing firms had been established, and six distinctive styles began to develop.

The 'Bow Top' caravan adhered to the simplest form of design and featured a rudimentary waggon with chenille canvas roof over a hooped wooden frame. Front and rear walls of tongue-in-groove panelling gave strength to the overall structure with a wooden access door provided at the front.

The 'Open Lot' or 'Yorkshire Bow' was almost identical in appearance to the 'Bow Top' but instead of the wooden panel and door at the front, there was just a curtain affording at least some level of privacy for the occupants.

Besides the canvas roof caravans were four types of entirely wooden construction.

By 1870, carriage makers, Dunton & Sons, had begun building the 10ft long 'Reading'. Taking the identity of the company's home town, it featured a tapered profile whereby the side walls sloped from a narrow floor up and out four inches to an arched roof, the appearance earning it the nickname, 'Kite Waggon'. Both exterior and interior were lavishly finished with mirrors, rich marquetry and gold leaf (or gold paint), and the living area benefited from built-in storage space.

The entrance door and removable steps were located at the front between the harnessing shafts whilst at the rear was a window with a hay rack or 'cratch' beneath, and both ends gained some protection from inclement weather with an extended roof supported by ornate brackets. Light from the side windows was further enhanced by a glazed lantern or 'mollicroft' roof. Typically, 'Readings' had front wheels of 3ft 6in diameter and rears of 5ft diameter to cope with the rough unpaved roads of the day. In recent times, 'Readings' have proved the most sought after of all 'gypsy' caravans and return high prices at sale or auction.

The 'Ledge' was of a similar design to the 'Reading' but could be identified by the tapered sides stepped in over the wheels (hence the name) giving a much narrower floor. Over the wheels a cage made of carved spindles would be used to keep vegetables or bantams.

Most popular among travelling showmen and the Romanichal was the 'Burton', which began as a very plain-sided 'van with comparatively small wheels. Over time, the design gained ribbed outer framework of carved wood and fine decorative

Above Left: 'Burton' style horse-drawn van showing the superb level of craftsmanship in its construction.

Above: An 1890s example of the 'Reading' style horse-drawn vans that were being manufactured by Dunton & Sons, Reading, from the mid-19th Century.

paintwork and eventually became the most expensive type of 'gypsy' caravan available – the level of embellishment and type of 'van was often a good indication of a family's standing in the Romany community.

Finally the 'Brush' was of a type that today is represented by only one or two survivors. Used by itinerant vendors, it took its name from the wares the owners made and sold to earn a living, and was distinctive not only for the roof racking that carried brooms, baskets, mats and of course brushes between trading stops, but also for the rear entrance door and removable steps.

It was not uncommon for a reasonably sized family to exist whilst constantly on the move, demonstrating innovative and sometimes quite astonishing ways to convey their entire worldly possessions within the small confines of a single living van. Up until the outbreak of World War I, showman John Beach travelled around Ireland with a four-wheel caravan he had built in 1895. In side lockers were carried all the elements to construct a coconut shy, and Beach would spend the season earning a pittance by following the fair from town to town. The living area was sparsely appointed with a wood burning stove and limited cupboard space. Towards the rear was a single-sized cabin bed which seems to have been adequate enough accommodation to sleep Beach's entire family of five – the children using the cupboard under the bed!

Genuine original horse-drawn caravans are a rare breed. Before the value in restoring and preserving Britain's heritage was truly realised, it was an age-old tradition for a Romany caravan owned by a gypsy chief to be burnt once its owner had passed on. Thankfully, not all examples met their end in this way and some were put out to grass in quiet corners of barns, fields and yards and left to rot. Today, there is a dedicated band of enthusiasts determined to save all existing 'vans for the enjoyment and education of future generations.

Below: Still in use today, this 'Bowtop' was pictured near Ringwood, Hampshire in 2011.

The Gentleman Gypsy

The point in time at which the idea of using a horse-drawn caravan as practical accommodation and means

of carrying goods to sell can really only be estimated, but the origins of caravanning as a way of holidaying is rather better documented. Late Victorian Britain was in the throes of the Industrial Revolution and many cities were choking with acrid smoke and fumes that spewed from the mills, workshops and factories. All level of society living and working within the manufacturing heartlands were prone to ill health but it would be a long time, in fact not until the late-1930s, that statutory holiday pay would become law. Despite the Bank Holidays Act being passed by the British Government in 1871, this entitled workers to just an extra four

Above: The Wanderer caravan pictured with W. Gordon Stables, his children and crew.

days rest in England, Wales and Ireland, and five in Scotland. Only those of certain means and the time to do so could take their leave in the country or at seaside resorts.

Owners of hotels and boarding houses began to enjoy lucrative earnings from the well-to-do yet there were still the more adventurous who preferred to take their vacation in less indulgent surroundings and fully enjoy the 'Great Outdoors'. One such person was Dr William Gordon Stables, an author and former surgeon in the Royal Navy who recognised the health advantages of holidaying in the open air. He was particularly taken by the gypsy lifestyle and in

1884 commissioned the Bristol Wagon & Carriage Works Limited to build a horse-drawn caravan of a size and type usually employed by travelling preachers and religious organisations. At 18ft long and over 6ft wide, it was constructed of mahogany and fitted with such congenial luxuries as a sofa bed, pantry, Rippingille oil stove and even a pianola! A year after

taking delivery, Stables, a native of Aberchirder, Banffshire in Scotland, who in retirement had settled at Twyford, Berkshire, embarked on an expedition back to his homeland and in so doing, unwittingly ignited a craze for leisure caravanning. The return journey covered 1,300 miles and with a coachman driving and a valet riding ahead on a tricycle ensuring their

route was unobstructed, Stables was able to sit back, enjoy the ride and take inspiration from the changing countryside to write his musings. He referred to his caravan as a 'land yacht', christening it The Wanderer and indeed his book Cruise of the Land Yacht, Wanderer or 1,300 Miles in My Caravan records the journey. Another of his publications was entitled The Gentleman Gypsy, a term adopted by those who championed holidaying by caravan, though Stables would also refer to his fellow travellers as 'Amateur Gypsies' or 'Caravanists'.

Early leisure caravanning was very much a pastime for more affluent individuals and those taking up the hobby would often find themselves hobnobbing with the hoi polloi.

Car and Caravan or Car-Caravan?

In the late-1800s, with the invention of the internal combustion engine, a new mode of transport hit the streets. The autocar rapidly attracted enthusiasm among aristocratic hot-heads and keen engineers alike and as these early fragile and unwieldy contraptions gradually gave way to more reliable, controllable models, 'autocarists' were able to confidently undertake journeys of ever greater distance with only minimal repair and maintenance. By the turn of the Century, however, those of creative and mechanical minds had found all manner of ways to utilise what was essentially a direct replacement to the horse or horse and carriage. With motor cars and leisure caravans first making their presence on Britain's roads at about the same time, it was logical to some enterprising individuals that the two ideas should be combined. For a number of years, there appeared in the motoring press many experimental do-it-yourself vehicles built specifically for touring and holidaying that could provide a degree of home comforts whilst preserving some of the rustic charm of camping.

The term 'car-caravan' was coined during the mid-1900s and referred to a wooden frame and panelled living van style body attached to a large car or light commercial vehicle chassis. One of the first was exhibited at the 1904

Paris Salon, a 40hp De Dietrich fitted with a handsome Pullman-style body and equipped with beds, seats, writing table, electric lighting and bells, and a dressing room.

In 1912, an article in Autocar magazine detailed a similar vehicle built at the Prescot home of Mr & Mrs G. A. Gamble. With a 14hp Star car chassis as a starting point, Mr Gamble had used traditional gypsy caravan construction techniques complete with mollicroft lantern roof and rear entrance door to create a neat but somewhat heavy vehicle with a high centre of gravity. Power to weight ratio was always a

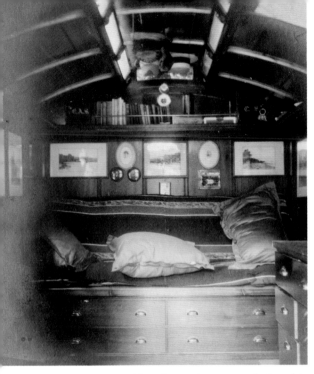

Above: Evidence of fine carpentry and furniture making abound in the interior of this typical pre-War touring 'van.

Centre: The first meeting of the Caravan Club of Great Britain & Ireland at Ockham, Surrey in 1908.

problem for engines never designed to pull such loads and indeed, on a tour of the Scottish Highlands, that covered hundreds of miles, Mr Gamble's Star could only average between 12 and 18mph. Great interest was generated from such exercises with any 'car-caravan' demonstrating reasonable performance or fuel consumption.

The following year there was an in-depth article on another chap's efforts using a 13.9hp Stoewer chassis. Although this vehicle resembled little more than a delivery van, the owner had at least considered the weight issue by using an ash frame panelled with plywood and had chosen to kit the interior out with only the most basic and essential equipment. Behind the driver's cab, the living area measured just 6ft x 5ft and appeared to contain all the comforts of a prison

cell – towel rail and coat hooks, a rear window with curtains, electric lighting and a fold-away wash basin with mirror. Side benches could be converted into a double bed and, with the body weighing just 5cwt, an average of 21mpg had been recorded over the 5,040 miles covered since construction. Canvas canopies were attached to either side of the vehicle when encamped and it was this feature that prompted a letter in a subsequent issue to suggest that these draughty open shelters (that, quite frankly, would offer no protection during stormy weather), could make adequate accommodation for the chauffeur or

Above: J. Harris Stone, 1853-1939, founder of the Caravan Club of Great Britain & Ireland.

indeed "the 'servant-interpreter' who would prove indispensable in out-of-the-way districts"! The letter was written by Mr Elwes and, interestingly, it highlighted some of the physical problems endured – and perhaps requiring consideration – during the early days of touring. He indicated that such a vehicle's wheel track should be of a width comparable with age-old channelled cart tracks and that the engine must have sufficient ground clearance so as to pass unimpaired over ruts, fords and standing water.

Prior to World War I, horse-drawn caravanning had continued to attract a good following and as early as 1907 eleven enthusiasts met at the London home of fellow caravanner, J. Harris Stone, and formed The Caravan Club of Great Britain & Ireland. Its objective was to issue helpful information to like-minded people, such as news on the latest camping products or location of suitable campsites (although it would be almost thirty years before the first Caravan Club Directory of Sites was published). The Club also

Above: Frederick Alcock's 1914 streamlined caravan is believed to be the first built for towing behind a car, in this case Mr Alcock's 1913 38hp Lanchester.

committed to organising gatherings to build a social community and the very first of these was held in May 1908 in a meadow at Ockham, Surrey. By the time the Club had attended its second rally just over a year later in Cranford Bridge, Middlesex, membership had risen to 157.

The idea of towing a trailer-type caravan behind a car is thought to have been pioneered by Frederick Alcock in 1914. His graceful caravan was very advanced for its day with streamlined roof and a central axle, and should have inspired other enthusiasts to emulate the design had it not been for the outbreak of World War I. With war came an urgent need to supply troops on the front line and J. Harris Stone of The Caravan Club of Great Britain & Ireland rallied members to relinquish their horse-drawn 'vans for the war effort. Many were sent forward after conversion to Red Cross ambulances, command posts and field kitchens. Towards the end of the conflicts, the Allied troops were pursuing a rapidly retreating and demoralised German army and Field Marshal Haig requested another batch of caravans to aid the advance. In just 24 hours, Harris Stone had amassed another fifty caravans and dispatched them across the English Channel. He had also used his own money to fund some of the Club's achievements during the conflicts and by September 1918 was owed £8 in expenses. It would be a while before he was reimbursed, however, as at the time the Club's own reserves stood at just £3!

After the War, a lively debate ensued in the motoring press comparing the virtues of the motor caravan against those of the car-towed caravan. It was argued that the motor caravan, typically of larger engine capacity could be quicker to drive, was instantaneously set up on site, demonstrated little difficulty when manoeuvring, and apart from cross winds, rarely suffered the problems such as tail-wobble that caravanners often experienced. On the other hand, the car-towed caravan could be pitched on site, belongings securely stowed on board, and the car could then be conveniently driven away on local excursions without the need to bring everything along for the ride!

Disputing the same pros and cons has continued right up to the present day!

Ello Eccles!

When the Armistice was finally declared in 1919, the armed forces realised they had a large surplus of vehicles, equipment and raw materials to dispose of, a lot of which had been sent across the Atlantic by the United States to help the war effort. Many soldiers returning to Blighty had during the conflicts been forced to adapt and learn new skills in the harsh conditions of trench warfare and were keen to use their new-found talents in the emergent manufacturing industries on home soil. The public were also determined to put behind them the austerity that had beset Europe and elsewhere during the previous five years.

First to reignite interest in holidaying by caravan was Captain St Barbe Baker. He constructed a canvas sided four-wheeler on the lines of a gypsy 'Burton' style 'van using redundant aeroplane parts and, realising some potential, went into production as the Navarac Caravan Company. The venture only lasted a year but already others had followed Baker's lead and started manufacture.

Left: A
1958-vintage
Eccles pictured in
the classic caravan
display at the Great
Dorset Steam Fair.

Although convenient for the travelling showman or, in the case of steam roller crew, suitable overnight lodgings between shifts on road construction, the four-wheeler was, however, already regarded out of date. Frederick Alcock's pre-War caravan was an inspiration, and companies such as the Stockport-based concern, Angela, and G. Hay-Moulder's Grosvenor of Chelsea were soon displaying their own ideas based on the single centre-axle concept.

In Birmingham, the Riley family who had constructed a home-made motor caravan in 1913, joined forces with The Eccles Transport Company. After a year of servicing the Eccles lorry fleet, Bill Riley Jnr suggested producing a variety of enclosed trailers as a side line having, as a service man with the Royal Flying Corps, witnessed their versatility on the front line during World War I. Bill Snr was not so confident and favoured a return to motor caravan production. The father and son team, both on the Eccles Board of Directors, could not agree and decided instead to gauge public opinion. One trailer and one motor caravan were completed and, though

not deemed appropriate exhibits for the 1919 Motor Show, were instead put on full view in a garage on the approach to the Show. Although many expressed a passing interest, only one order was taken for the trailer caravan, the customer being none other than Welsh suffragette, feminist and philanthropist, Sybil Thomas, Viscountess Rhondda of Llanwern. A single purchase may have seemed scant reward for the time and effort it took to build the caravan, but the publicity generated from this sale alone was enough incentive to begin serious production. It was decided to put the transport business on hold and make a batch of fifty, concentrating all workforce on trailer manufacture. Their Birmingham premises, however,

could not sufficiently cope with this level of output and the William Turner firm from nearby Cradley Heath were subcontracted to make the body shells. These were then sent back to Eccles for finishing with interior detail and their own pattern axles.

Promoted as a trailer range addressing different private and commercial needs that included mobile shops, portable health centres and of course holiday accommodation, Eccles were still finding their feet and their early leisure caravans were of simple steel sheet construction with spartan interior. By the early-1920s, they had developed their construction techniques and the designs embraced more home comforts.

Ever enthusiastic, the company had foreseen growth potential within the market, choosing not only to advertise their own range but to also promote the virtues of holidaying by caravan. Part of their strategy was a road campaign undertaken by Bill Riley Jnr who used a standard Eccles 'van and 1910 Rover as tow-car to tour the country and demonstrate the caravan's numerous attributes. In doing so, Riley was also able to fully test the product for himself and convey any improvements or indeed sensible suggestions from the public back to the factory in Birmingham.

Robust support legs at each corner did away with a hitherto necessity to use guy ropes, pneumatic tyres and an improved car-to-caravan coupling system were all innovative, and the stylish 'cottage' exterior inspired other companies to join the industry. As the membership of The Caravan Club continued to climb, Eccles began to enjoy steady sales with mounting orders. With the public's yearning for post-War leisure and recreation, they were soon industry leaders and in 1927 opened the first factory dedicated purely to caravan production complete with modern machinery and a blacksmith shop. This was at Stirchley and was built on a four-acre site with enough potential for future expansion.

Commercial 'vans and horse boxes made up a large proportion of output from Eccles' Stirchley site with

Above: Everyone wanted to do their bit for the war effort and Caravan Club member, Mrs Fowler, is pictured in 1942 with her Eccles 'First Aid Post' caravan The Bluebird.

promotional campaign groups and religious organisations making up a significant sector of customers. Buoyed by this flourishing side of the business, the company was able to concentrate on leisure 'van development and in so doing became the largest manufacturer of caravans in the world, selling not only to aspiring holiday makers, but to showmen and Romany folk as well. Chassis were now made in-house and with each caravan encompassing a variety of build techniques and materials the 15,000 square feet of factory floor boasted a diverse workforce of craftsmen.

From Boom to Gloom – The Industry Between the Wars

Not all wishing to holiday by caravan could afford the cost of purchase and so as not to deny them the pleasure, many companies entered the caravan hire business operating and maintaining fleets throughout the year. One of the first to do so was Bertram Hutchings who, after nurturing a love of caravanning by spending his honeymoon in a horse-drawn four-wheeler, decided to start small scale manufacture and hire them out. These were lightweight vehicles capable of being pulled by a single horse. Hutchings had also dabbled in motor caravan production and when war broke out in 1914, some of these were pressed into military service. In 1919, Hutchings was inspired by advances in caravan development, primarily by Eccles and launched his own range of single-axle two-wheelers. He still continued to build horse-drawn vehicles right up to the 1930s and blended many traditional gypsy 'van idiosyncrasies into his two-wheel products. The Hutchings Voyager was a case in point, a very upright design complete with lantern roof and bay windows, although the top-heavy look was somewhat alleviated by a low ride height. The Hutchings Tom Thumb introduced towards the end of the 1920s addressed this problem further. It was built to a height of just under 6ft but once pitched on site featured a floor that could be lowered, thus increasing headroom. For this to be possible the normal straight

Above: In 1919, Bertram Hutchings began building two-wheel centre-axle caravans intended for towing behind a car, in this case the ubiquitous Ford Model T.

beam or cranked axle usually featured on caravans of the day was dispensed with and, instead, the chassis cleverly incorporated independent leaf spring suspension. A de-Luxe version called the Lady Nimble was later added to the catalogue.

Construction techniques steadily progressed throughout the 1920s and '30s. In the early years, the use of wooden chassis was common practice with side panels and roofs of canvas covered plywood on an ash or oak frame. The canvas was made waterproof to prevent warping and with traditional carpentry providing the interior fittings, it all made for a very heavy vehicle. As time went by the wooden chassis was replaced by riveted or welded steel and the body shop made greater use of fibreboard. Some manufacturers went a step further cladding the outer skin with aluminium sheeting thoughtfully finished with a cheerful colour scheme.

With many caravanners choosing to purchase their own examples and with the large fleets of caravans available for hire, the industry was well-established by the end of the 1920s. The hitherto rare chance of finding a dedicated campsite was slowly being redressed by enterprising farmers with land to spare, and the motoring press were offering greater coverage to caravan-related products. Featured stories often told of the extraordinary distances some intrepid owners would cover or the extreme terrain encountered in a single tour, and detailed expeditions across continents and deserts, through uncharted territory and delightful ascents high up into glaciated

mountain ranges. As caravanners became more adventurous and determined come rain or shine to use their 'vans throughout the year, the manufacturers responded by installing gas heaters and hot and cold

Above: A campsite near the North Wales coastal village of Dyffryn-Ardudwy, circa 1937.

Left: Caravan touring 1920s-style! The car is a Vauxhall D-Type.

running water, whilst double-skin walls, roofs and floors were introduced and all insulated with various materials.

In 1932, Autocar magazine held their first caravan rally in Minehead, Somerset, attracting 93 entrants for the various competitions – among them a good number of manufacturers such as Carlight, Red Rics, Shadow and Ensor, and of course Eccles and Hutchings. At the time, it ranked as a major event with well-known motoring personalities joining the judging panel, including pioneer racing driver, S. F. Edge, and Autocar illustrator, F. Gordon Crosby. There were prizes for the best designs in two, three, four and more berth caravans, camping trailers (or 'trailer tents' as the equivalent is known today), collapsible caravans and car-caravans (motor caravans).

It was noted that many of the competing tow-cars were equipped with spare wheels shod with 'mud grips' to prevent wheel spin through well-used and muddy gateways – a particular problem in the early days of touring. Another annoyance of the early caravanner was getting one's hands soiled when hitching the 'van to the car! Hand cleaning products were often already stowed away ahead of the journey and to ease the task of removing any sticky residue from one's hands and avoid staining clothing, W. A. Woods of North Devon seriously suggested lubricating the towing hitch with butter!

The Minehead rally was a tremendous success, reportedly one of gaiety and much merriment with impromptu cocktail parties, the air filled with gramophone music and from dawn 'til dusk, endless but jovial discussions about the multitude of innovative devices on show, designed to aid the caravanner's vacation.

In the days before the invention of the portable chemical loo, very few caravans were furnished with a lavatory as there was very little room within the living space to provide adequate privacy or, indeed, sound insulation!

Instead, small toilet tents complete with bench seating were pitched over freshly dug holes at the edge of the field, and as far as way and downwind from the 'van as was physically possible! There was on the rare occasion, however, a manufacturer who would attempt to lure customers to purchase their product with the added promise of on-board toilet facilities. Lewis & Richards of Royston, Fairway of Llandudno and the Colchester firm of Essex were all early exponents but the concept was never a popular one, and it was not until the invention of the removable waste cartridge that the idea became reasonably bearable.

In 1933, Caravan And Trailer, the world's first magazine dedicated to car-hauled vehicles was launched by Mit Harris and Bernard Dolman. This was the forerunner of the Caravan Magazine that, today, is said to have a larger readership than some of the leading celebrity gossip magazines. Harris and Dolman would prove

instrumental to the survival of The Caravan Club when in 1935 they took over its management from an aging J. Harris Stone who it seems had been abandoned to run the organisation almost single-handedly. Having founded the Club twenty-eight years earlier, Harris Stone stepped back and became Vice-President. The Club was re-launched as a limited company and Harris and Dolman used their Caravan And Trailer magazine to good effect, encouraging readers to join. At that time, membership had dwindled to 80 but in just two years this number had swelled to 1,300! Within three years, however, Harris and Dolman had fallen out and sold all Caravan Club

and Caravan And Trailer assets to the publishing group, Link House.

1937 saw the inauguration of a members club for owners of Winchester caravans. It may have been short-lived – only lasting a year – but inspired many to follow suit in later and, as events in Europe would soon dictate, happier times.

With the threat of invasion from Hitler's Germany on the horizon and a real possibility that leisure time was about to be cut and fuel rationed, Club members were unsurprisingly prompted to make the most of what precious free time they had left. Over 200 caravans arrived for the 1939 National Rally held near Northampton, a record number of attendees before Europe and the rest of the world were plunged once again into war.

The '30s had proved a boom era for the caravan industry with the best part of a hundred companies in manufacture. Many would not survive the conflicts but when peace returned it was a chance for new thinking and a new breed.

The Streamliners

In the late-1920s, caravan design generally followed two schools of thought. On the one hand, there were those with the traditional square profile that offered utilitarian living space, generous headroom and decent storage facilities, and then there were the streamliners with design emphasis on sleek body styling but often to the detriment of practicality. Nevertheless, with many owners securing semi-permanent pitches for their conventional caravans to limit the tricky task of manoeuvring, the streamliner became the preferred choice of those wanting to roam, and the type was soon referred to as the 'tourer'.

Today, as par for the course, caravans incorporate aerodynamic devices to aid the flow of air when towed at speed and are very much a safety consideration, but caravans built between the Wars were less prone to enter a tail-wobble or at worse overturn. By law, the speed at which a caravan should be towed remained at a snail's pace right up to 1963 when the limit was increased to the dizzy heights of 40mph.

Streamlining in the 1920s and '30s was all about the aesthetics! Coachbuilders and stylists in the motor industry had already introduced attractive tear-drop, beetle-back, boat and wasp tail, profiling to automobile bodywork and the ideas soon brushed off on those in the leisure trailer industry.

Bertram Hutchings was first to usher in the concept with his Winchester of 1930. With a dramatic full-length sweeping roofline, curvaceous front and rear panels and a two-tone colour scheme, it was an instant hit and a real head-turner for its day. The arc of the roof meant that headroom and the size of the windows were compromised at either end, but the Winchester proved to be a trend-setting exercise and prompted Eccles and the Chiswick-based company,

Car Cruiser, to follow suit.

Eccles' response was the rather lacklustre Ecclelite which attempted to keep pace with the new thinking but was not as outlandish as the Winchester and with its token curved roof and boxy shell still retained a very conservative appearance. But Eccles had built a reputation as Britain's leading caravan manufacturer and it was not long before they had caught up.

Major Clifford Fleming-Williams

Above: A 1930s Winchester Royal – 'the Rolls-Royce of caravans'.

was a World War I artist whose illustrations were regularly published in the British press conveying the harsh conditions under which the Allies fought. His passion, however, lay in the wind-cheating dynamics of the aeroplane fuselage as he had already shown what could be achieved by building a very modern looking motor caravan, christening it Car Cruiser. After the War, he focussed on applying

aviation thinking to caravan design and built the first example in 1920. It generated so much interest that Fleming-Williams was encouraged to commence production, adopting Car Cruiser for the company name. Car Cruiser caravans displayed very attractive detailing that included Art Deco inspired 'sunrise' window panels and interior upholstery. Structurally they were built to the highest standard,

Above: A 1930s
Winchester Royal
– 'the Rolls-Royce
of caravans'.

almost entirely of wood including the bulk of the chassis, and later models featured a double skin laminated roof to reduce the formation of condensation. As demand grew, Major Fleming-Williams was compelled to find larger factory premises and eventually all proceedings were moved to Hayes in Middlesex.

Amongst the other companies whose designs were greatly influenced by the aviation industry were Bob Earl's Sleaford-based firm Carlight Caravans, the Silver Ball range of Lewis & Reed of Royston, Hertfordshire, and Atlas Trailers & Caravans of Chelmsford.

Earl had recognised the strengthening properties of interior storage units and used them to great effect reducing the amount of supporting framework to the body panels and thus saving weight.

Atlas, on the other hand, pushed

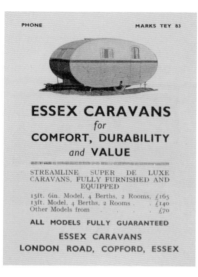

PHONE   MARKS TEY 83

ESSEX CARAVANS
for
COMFORT, DURABILITY
and VALUE

STREAMLINE SUPER DE LUXE
CARAVANS, FULLY FURNISHED AND
EQUIPPED

15ft. 6in. Model, 4 Berths, 2 Rooms, £165
13ft. Model, 4 Berths, 2 Rooms . . £140
Other Models from £70

ALL MODELS FULLY GUARANTEED

ESSEX CARAVANS
LONDON ROAD, COPFORD, ESSEX

the boundaries of aerodynamics with their fantastically wacky Aerovan. Introduced in 1934, it is said to have taken inspiration from another form of transport popular at the time, the airship, and did indeed display a bulbous nose not unlike that of the great zeppelins. Teardrop-profile spats covered the wheels and with an overall height of just 5ft 4in, it was designed to fit neatly into existing motor car garages. The model was aimed directly at the sportscar enthusiast but whether many were sold is doubtful as the Aerovan only possessed interior headroom of 4ft 4in!

Car Cruiser were now in direct

ESSEX
CARAVANS
The Best in the World

15ft. "Princess," 4 Berths, 2 Rooms £155
16ft. 6in. Super de Luxe. Very latest design £289

ESSEX CARAVANS
Copford, Colchester : Phone: Marks Tey 83

Northern Distributors: HARRINGTON & CO., DELAMERE FOREST DEPOT, OAKMERE, CHESHIRE
Southern Distributors: LAND YACHTS LTD., ORMONDE LODGE, ENGLEFIELD GREEN, SURREY

competition with Eccles, Winchester and Cheltenham – yet another company whose products had become renowned for quality of workmanship.

The Colchester–based firm, in Essex, wowed visitors at the 1933 Motor Show with the Monarch. It took elegant styling to a new height with its flowing lines, from the continuous curved front panel, up over the lantern roof and down to a rising ducktail. It incorporated a number of up-to-date features including sliding doors, fitted radio and self-levelling corner legs, and was reasonably priced at £275.

Arguably the most distinctive designs to come out of the 1930s were the Royal and Swallow made by the Airlite Trailer Co., Ltd at the Old Meteor Works, Coventry. The Royal was advertised as "…the caravan of your dreams" and, depicted in an illustration being pulled by a Rolls-Royce Twenty, was described as the "Queen of the Road". The stylish outer skin of steel-bonded construction eliminating any exterior beading and adorned with a graceful sweeping waist band was the brainchild of ex-SS employee, Clifford Dawltrey – SS in this instance referring to nothing

more sinister than William Lyons' car manufacturing firm, successor to Swallow Sidecars and forerunner of Jaguar. A triple layer of Sundeala

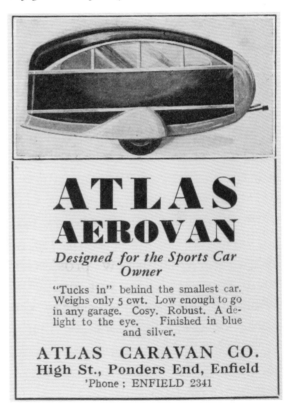

semi-insulated hardboard, Insulite and French polished oak was used for each of the Royal's walls and the body sat on a steel chassis fabricated in-house. By the mid-1930s, proprietary chassis were available from specialist firms including Brockhouse, Dixon-Bate, Leason and Wadsworth and although small concerns such as Adams, Monksgate and Taylor took advantage of a ready-made basis on which to

build their own design coachwork, Airlite emphatically dismissed this as an option. There were even plans to put into production an Airlite car but, unfortunately, the name did not even survive to the outbreak of World War II and in 1938 Clifford Dawltrey turned his attention to a new venture, Coventry Steel Caravans Ltd.

In a 1937 magazine supplement which promoted the Airlite Royal, the

virtues of the caravan were fanatically expounded, but already the article alluded to the threat of war. It was obvious there were growing public concerns as to the menacing behaviour of Hitler's Werhmacht and a quote from an Airlite customer working alongside the Ministry of Defence suggested that it was not scare-mongering to expect air-raids in the near future. By purchasing a caravan, he had planned for such eventualities and would be able to escape the city with his family to "a secluded nook of the countryside". Just a couple of years later, his prophecy was alarmingly accurate and although the early-1940s saw most caravan manufacturers employed in the production of munitions and military equipment, a number were commissioned to build relief accommodation for displaced evacuees.

Above: A 1930s Car Cruiser with rudimentary improvements to the roof. Scenes like this were common during World War II when displaced evacuees were forced to live in caravans due to bombing raids on large British cities.

Post-War Austerity

During the dark days of World War II, any hope of a family holiday had to be put on hold and understandably there were few orders taken for new leisure caravans. Many established companies such as Winchester and Car Cruiser were commandeered into helping the war effort and Eccles, for example, turned their skills to building ambulances, searchlight vehicles and mobile offices.

The world was changing considerably and there came an immediate and urgent need to house a large number of displaced people evacuated from London and other industrial cities that had suffered bombing during the Blitz. The answer came in the form of hurriedly designed and crudely constructed caravans that were dispatched to areas where they were most needed. As a result, shanty towns sprang up containing demoralised and destitute families from all backgrounds, thrown together and forced to make the best out of a desperate situation. This was not a short-term solution as even by 1950, it was estimated that 80 per cent of caravan manufacturing output was intended for residential use. The unavailability of quality build materials nationwide and a lack of good insulation meant that residents were ill-equipped for the vagaries of a British winter and when in 1945 peace was finally restored, the caravan industry had

Above: A Fairholme Bambi two-berth caravan and Rover 90.

an unfavourable reputation to dispel.

Nevertheless, Eccles were ready for the challenge and eager to return to the boom years of leisure caravanning. The 'flow-line' assembly technique they had used in 1939 for their National model was again put into practice and the Birmingham company were soon up to speed producing the 14ft Enterprise. Demand was surprisingly high and in the first 18 months of manufacture, 500 examples left the works. The pace at which caravans could now be churned out had been boosted enormously by wartime developments in glues. Jig-assembly, a method already put into practice in 1924 by Balmforth of Yorkshire, was becoming widespread and sections for front, side and rear panels were individually and identically made on a jig before stockpiling prior to final assembly.

The days of the elegant and sumptuous hand-built tourers were,

Above: One of many styles of caravan at the time being driven to its destination.

Henry and Sam Alper had bought a job lot of redundant Supermarine Spitfire aircraft landing and tail wheels and cleverly utilised them on the Rover's central axle and towing hitch jockey-wheel respectively. Little could anyone predict that from this first model, Sam Alper would go on to build a huge multi-national empire and dominate caravan production throughout the three subsequent decades. The story was extremely important in the history of British caravanning and will be the subject of the next chapter.

Another firm to benefit from the aviation industry – this time providing skilled labour – was F. G. Bailey Ltd of Bristol. In 1948, Martin Bailey, an ex-employee of the Bristol Aircraft Company turned his hand to the construction of caravans. He had already found a niche market in making furniture of a quality and price the people of post-War Britain could afford, and by combining his carpentry skills with those learned as a sheet metal worker during the War was able to create the first in a long line of excellent caravans. This was the Maestro and, advertised for £300, represented very good value for money for a five-berth.

unfortunately, gone forever. In their place came a squarer more utilitarian form of caravan and as build materials continued to be in short supply or rationed, it was a time of much improvisation.

The Streamlite Rover was announced in 1947. It displayed a very attractive and rather purposeful road stance with low ground clearance, a straight line side skirt unbroken along its entire length due to spats over the wheels, and a splendid 270 degree panoramic view from the front dinette. Its creators,

For the time being, one material that seemed to be available in abundance was aluminium and the caravan industry was quick to take advantage. It soon proved problematic as manufacturers not used to the distorting properties of aluminium at different temperatures, were treating it as a direct replacement to the plywood and hardboard panels used for caravan bodywork before the War. By the time hardboard sheets had become more readily available again, designers had realised that it was a poor substitute unable to sustain the longevity of other materials such as aluminium, and chose to incorporate a combination of both materials into new models.

North of the border in the Falkirk district of Carron, Thomson, were ranking second only to Eccles in terms of size and output. Thomson were set up in 1908 as a Cartwright but began manufacturing showmen's living vans. By 1924, the company was hiring out a fleet of single-axle leisure caravans and through steady expansion and

Above: A caravan park of the late-1940s clearly showing the sort of low quality 'vans appearing after the dark days of World War II that tended to give the industry a bad name.

Above: Folding caravans being loaded on board a cargo ship, ready for export to the Continent.

Birmingham rivals, Eccles.

Enthusiasm for caravanning had not, it seemed, diminished during the conflicts and membership of The Caravan Club continued to steadily rise so that by 1947, it stood at over 4,200. With the advances in construction methods came an influx of new manufacturers, more often than not set up by individuals previously employed by others in the Establishment. This was very much evident at the 1948 Motor Show where innovation and new thinking was mixed with the products of the traditionalists. The trouble was that some companies with years of experience behind them were slow to use state-of-the-art techniques and materials, and it took many a while to conform. By then, potential customers had been lured away by the newcomers and the reputation and standing of the 'old guard' was soon found to be under threat. Eccles were one such casualty and no longer commanded the respect they enjoyed during the inter-war years. Whilst the likes of Eccles, Winchester and Cheltenham tried to catch up, companies such as Bailey, Paladin and Safari had seized opportunity, offering affordable caravans to a public eager to

by ensuring their products kept pace with the trends of the day, Thomson eventually became the leading caravan manufacturer in Scotland. Where many companies fell by the wayside especially during World War II, Thomson diversified and, like other prudent and far-sighted visionaries, turned their hand to essential supply of military equipment. To cope with demand, they took over another local firm, Scott Roadcraft, and by the end of the War were worthy competition to their overcome post–War austerity and start enjoying themselves again. The Bailey Maestro, for example, had become so popular that the company would soon need to find larger premises to cope with demand. Car Cruiser were one of the pre-War firms that quickly adapted their manufacturing style in line with contemporary trends unveiling the very modern Adelphi at the Motor Show.

By 1950, it was recorded that over 400 caravan manufacturers had begun trading since the end of the War, and that was in the UK alone! The next few years, however, saw that figure gradually decrease by approximately a third as ill-conceived, over-ambitious and under-financed projects fell by the wayside.

A sizeable number of 1950s caravans were dreadfully functional in appearance as demonstrated by the Avalon range. The severely boxy exterior of the their 22ft Everest model, for example, lacked any hint of tasteful styling with, it seems, only a modicum of consideration having gone into the two-tone paint job!

In Sherborne, Dorset, grocer Les Bennett had decided to build his own caravan for personal use and like many before him designed it without first studying contemporary practice. The

Above: Caravans could be used for holidays or just family picnics in the park.

result was a two-ton albatross of a thing that could have done little for the tow-car's fuel economy and was more at home permanently located on site. Indeed, the Bennett's went into static home production as Castleton Caravans and the first eighteen examples were built by a workforce comprising simply of the Bennett husband and wife team. It was not until the end of the decade that a wholly satisfactory touring caravan was being displayed on the Castleton stand at Earls Court.

Nevertheless, there were still those whose passion and understanding of good design would stand them in good stead throughout the '50s and '60s. The era saw a vogue for the 'coach shape', largely square-sided caravans with ogee curves at each end, top and bottom. A 'V' peaked roofline also became popular and numerous models displayed both characteristics. Manufacturers also found ways of making caravans better appointed and it was a period when features such as electrically pumped hot and cold running water, gas or coal stoves, showers, baths, fold-away ironing boards, radios and clocks, and even rubbish chutes were all considered and often fitted as standard. With more indulgences included in the specification, the price inevitably rose and a healthy 'Luxury' market developed with Burlingham, Freeman, Kingston and Winchester leading the way. Winchester had, in fact, built up such a reputation for quality and opulence that it had earned the title 'The Rolls-Royce of Caravans'.

Eccles soldiered on and whilst the company was still held in high esteem for quality of workmanship, needed to keep afloat and entered the budget market with the Alert. Likewise, Bailey of Bristol announced the 11ft Maestro Minor, a 'van that would attract good sales from European buyers. By the mid-1960s, nearly half the output from Bailey was destined for overseas dealerships.

Poole in Dorset was as unlikely a place as anywhere to become a centre of caravan production yet, throughout the 1950s, a number of companies were established typically by ex-employees of Bluebird. This concern was founded in the mid-1930s by a youthful Bill Knott who with the financial support of his father was able to churn out inexpensive and relatively unremarkable caravans from his Parkstone premises. 'Unremarkable' might not have been a word chosen by some of his detractors as the build quality left a lot to be desired. In fact the key to Knott's early success lay in maintaining lower prices than his competitors and providing more people of lesser incomes the chance to join the steadily growing ranks of caravanners. This policy was most crucially continued after the War during the height of housing shortages and from auspicious sales, Knott was able to expand his range and start refining

the product. The improvements were widely reported in the caravan press and the hitherto dismissive attitude towards Bluebird Caravans slowly ebbed away as dealers became increasingly interested.

In 1963, after years of steady development and modest expansion, Bill Knott was approaching his fifties and decided that a change of direction was in order. He sold his shares in Bluebird and helped orchestrate a merger between the Bournemouth firm and one of its biggest rivals, Sprite.

By the late-1960s, the emphasis at the annual International Caravan Exhibition was beginning to turn in favour of mobile homes rather than touring 'vans, and more and more floor space at Earls Court was being devoted to static and semi-permanent holiday and residential accommodation. This was by no means reflecting a drop in sales or interest from the touring industry and indeed firms were striving at length to produce better caravans in terms of lightness in comparison to size, as well as stability under tow.

It was a period when the consideration for greater road safety became priority right across the motoring community. Whilst the old chassis firms of Witter and

Dixon Bate could still be found providing towing bracket kits, most caravan companies were choosing to use chassis from dedicated frame manufacturers such as Peak Trailers and B&B as a basis for construction, and nearly all ready-made chassis on offer had independent suspension fitted as standard, an element only optionally available during the mid-60s. B&B were one of the most popular manufacturers with chassis featuring Lockheed brakes and a universally used coupling system and for a while, B&B took the lion's share of the off-the-shelf chassis market until some companies began introducing their own frames fabricated in-house again towards the end of the 1970s.

The concept of a separate braking system in addition to that of the tow-car was, in the late 1960s, just starting to be introduced but overrun braking mechanisms had already become highly efficient with electrically operated versions appearing in ever greater numbers. With the effectiveness of two braking systems on a car and caravan outfit and the capability to stop in a much shorter time and distance, it reinforced the argument for increasing the speed limit of towing a caravan or trailer from the lumbering 40mph to something closer to the normal flow of traffic.

For a typical family car to be able to achieve an acceptable level of performance whilst towing, the optimum weight of the caravan was calculated as being no more than 75% of the car. But with nearly all 'vans being constructed of flat sheet panels over a wooden frame, it was extremely complicated and expensive for most

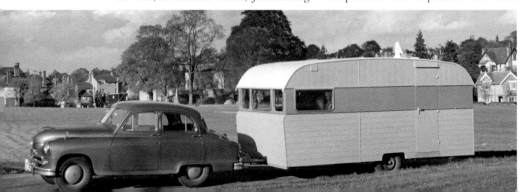

firms to come up with a wind-cheating aerodynamic shape. In some respects the squarer profile allowed the easier fitment of interior furnishings but with vehicles of less than 12ft in length, every inch of floor and wall space was made use of and naturally increased weight – yet these were the very caravans aimed at the small family runabout. With the introduction of resin bonded glass fibre for the exterior, a certain degree of effective streamlining could be considered with double curvatures moulded before final assembly. Problems of wind-resistance from flat fronted (and flat-rear) caravans were addressed and the Eccles Amethyst was one of the first to embrace the new technique with its flowing lines and modern looks by comparison to contemporary models.

By the 1970s, a shoddily and ill-conceived caravan that had been so prevalent fifteen or so years before was rarely reported and the British caravan industry was enjoying a reputation for high quality, right across the board.

The level of paraphernalia that an owner wished to have in their 'van was largely down to customer choice and the depth of purse. The motoring press encouraged prospective buyers not to go for the largest model they could afford or indeed the dearest within budget as it was often the case that some manufacturers certainly offered better value than those who were selling their products by name and established reputation alone. It was often better to buy the highest quality yet smallest caravan that could provide adequate and comfortable accommodation.

A claustrophobic living area could be

Below: A Ford Popular driver attracts an audience as he attempts a tricky U-turn manoeuvre. In tow is a Cresta built by one of many caravan firms started in Hull.

Above: A Dutch owned Bluebird Cambrian made in 1958.

greatly alleviated with the addition of a canvas awning and there were a number of tent manufacturers such as Blacks of Greenock, Joseph Bryant, S. T. Harrison and the Pneumatic Tent Company offering a range to fit all models of caravan.

During the 1960s and '70s there was a policy that caravan sites unable to provide a certain level of facility would only be certified to a limit of five 'vans pitched on site at any one time. A lack of dedicated sites across the country meant that booking was essential to avoid the disappointment and, in many instances, the desperation of being turned away.

Sam, the Sprite and CI

When Bluebird and Sprite merged in 1963, together they became the industry's largest manufacturer with the creation of Caravans International, or CI. Headed by Sam Alper, CI was a far cry from when he launched his first caravan project with the Streamlite Rover in 1947.

Alper had trained as an electrician with the Royal Navy's Fleet Air Arm and on demobilisation had joined brother Henry's new venture, Alperson Products, based in Stratford, London. The Rover was aimed at the average earner but benefited from slightly better quality of manufacture than the likes of Bluebird, and the cheerful and airy feel to the interior was greatly enhanced by a large opening skylight. Costs were kept to a minimum thanks to

the use of surplus Air Ministry materials including wheels and suspension from the Supermarine Spitfire, excess canvas from the production of barrage balloons for the roof, and for the superstructure, the Alper's tried using black bog oak dredged from the Fens – an extremely hardened and almost fossilised material. Following the success of this model, Alper introduced the Ranger and the Elf and sales began to take off.

In an attempt to attract sales to those of lesser means, the next model to emerge was the budget priced Streamlite Sprite. The first of these was simply constructed of tempered hardboard over a wooden frame representing an angular box with a curved roof, but its popularity was pivotal

Above: A 1960s publicity shot of a Sprite Countryman in tow behind the Wolseley 16/60.

to the fortunes of Alperson Products and its subsequent associated organisations.

Alper had gone to great lengths to understand the market and by talking to caravan enthusiasts as well as those who felt caravanning was financially beyond their capabilities, he was able to gauge the type of product that the market was lacking. Where Alper's rivals built caravans of a similar size and specification and priced them at over £500, the Sprite was capped at £200. It was an overnight success despite initial criticism to the standard of finish and, to meet demand, output was stepped up from one per week to an average of one per day.

North of the border, Thomson continued to expand and established themselves as Alper's biggest rival whilst Bluebird were the south's big hitters.

By 1952, Sprites were leaving the factory at a rate of 1,000 units per year and towards the end of the decade, production figures had more than doubled. Whilst the Sprite remained the mainstay of output, the catalogue boasted five other models tapping into the requirements of a wider customer base. They included the Alpine, Colt, Major and Musketeer and in little time at all, it was commonplace to see an Alperson caravan on British roads and campsites. With the Sprite becoming a

Above: A 1963
Sprite Alpine.

top-seller, it seemed logical to adopt the name for future company branding and 'Alperson Products' would in time be dropped in favour of 'Sprite Caravans'.

Sam Alper was himself a keen caravanning enthusiast and recognised the need for regular refreshment stops whilst driving to and from the campsites. In 1958, he opened the first of many small roadside diners that, located on busy 'A' roads, could cater for the weary traveller. The idea was based on American practice and the first example was opened near Reading in Berkshire. It was called Little Chef and in a relatively short time, a chain of restaurants were in operation the length and breadth of Britain.

With the dawning of a new decade and ever looking for opportunities to expand and command a greater slice of the market, Alper bought out the Eccles concern from Bill Riley in August 1960. That year, production was increased to over 5,000 units in response to the growing numbers taking up leisure caravanning and included a new model, the 400, designed for towage behind smaller family runabouts.

The firm had opened a new purpose-built state-of-the-art factory in Newmarket and to streamline output, the Eccles premises in Birmingham was closed

down and all processes moved to Suffolk. Eccles was always a brand renowned for dependable standards of construction but their image had become tired and somewhat staid. The move to Newmarket was the ideal opportunity for a fresh start and while retaining their luxury status, Eccles were re-launched with up-to-date styling ensuring their name endured into the future. Alper called upon former illustrator and furniture designer Reg Dean for the inspirational new look and his input almost single-handedly changed the direction of caravan interior design forever, typically using a combination of imitation teak and white vinyl to provide light, airy and decidedly refreshing accommodation. Over time, Dean's ideas would prove extremely influential and were applied to other models, not only for the companies that came under Alper's guardianship but, in later years, models of other firms keen to tap into Dean's visionary skills. The new Eccles range introduced a sloping front end and for a while, this feature distinctively set them apart from other 'vans on the market.

Expansion clearly bucked the trend over Alper's competitors with the early-1960s proving a difficult time for many. With recession taking a strangle hold on Britain's industries, a number of famous brands either disappeared from the scene or were swallowed by other firms. Paladin,

Siddall and Winchester were three of the casualties as was the former pace setting concern of Coventry Steel. Sprite might also have faltered when in 1961 a fire all but destroyed the factory paint shop. With the varying types of combustible material that went into making caravans, this was not an unusual occurrence and only three years before, F. G. Bailey of Bristol had suffered a similar catastrophe. Nevertheless, with a steadfast refusal to concede defeat, both companies had rallied the staff to improvise while repairs could be carried out.

Alongside the Sprite, the 400 progressively profited from a number of alterations and improvements and was one of the most popular models ever marketed, remaining in production for 16 years.

Output was at an all-time high with 10,000 units being dispatched from Newmarket in 1963. Reg Dean stayed

with the company until 1965 by which time Alper had bought the Poole-based firm Bluebird and the entire conglomerate had been re-branded as CI. The Bluebird range consisted of the Wren, Bantam, Dauphine and Europe and for a few years CI's income from the touring 'van market was enhanced by a pleasing level of sales from their Poole-based subsidiary. Eventually, however, Bluebird were instructed to concentrate on the construction of static homes leaving touring manufacture to other factories in the CI group. And indeed, the group was rapidly expanding. By the mid-1960s, CI were parent company to Eccles, Bluebird, Fairholme of Cardiff, South African firms Sprite Pty and Africaravans, and the West German concern of Wilk. The latter take-over caused something of a panic among Germany's other caravan manufacturers who colluded to form a cooperative aimed at preventing Alper taking a greater or at worst controlling stake in that country's caravan industry. CI, nevertheless, had established a foothold.

The 1963 merger meant that CI were now exporting to seventeen different countries worldwide, a factor that three years later brought Alper an audience with the Queen at Buckingham Palace, when he was awarded an OBE for services to British export.

Caravan production was, however, seasonal, concentrated very much during the spring, summer and autumn months. A natural lull would occur each winter and to avoid losing valuable staff and be forced to recruit again the following spring, Alper introduced a sideline in board games, sailing dinghies and prefabricated hotel rooms. The Newmarket factory was also the birthplace of the first golf buggy built on British soil which was subsequently

presented to President Eisenhower.

Eventually, popularity and intense demand would force the focus back to touring caravan production and the various sidelines of earlier years would be shelved. With the factory bursting as the seams, a second site was opened in the town enabling production to continue with Eccles and Fairholme at one site, and Sprite at the other. For a time, the different brands were developed independently and vehemently retained their own distinctive individuality. Innovative features implemented by one group might not, therefore, be immediately adopted by the others, but eventually each subsidiary was tasked with making particular standard fittings that could then be shared across the CI range.

By the end of the 1960s, CI had become the largest caravan manufacturer in the world employing over 1,000 staff and manufacturing 35,000 units per year. At the dawning of a new decade, CI were forced to increase their prices, yet still only moderately in comparison to their adversaries. Equipment and design across the CI range were greatly improved with Fairholme remaining their flagship brand in the luxury class and Eccles, Europa and

Centre: A Sprite Musketeer dating from circa 1973, pictured at the Great Dorset Steam Fair.

Sprite competing in the various touring categories. Fairholme caravans were all given names of finches and featured sleek body styling with a signature sloping front to the roof that addressed to some extent aerodynamics.

With the bulk of caravans built with aluminium panelling on a wooden frame, there developed an inevitable sameness, especially when viewed on a campsite. The crisp lines of the Eccles Amethyst must therefore have been a breath of fresh air. With its large window recessed into the front panel – an aspect that did little it seems to increase drag – the Amethyst would inspire further Eccles models such as the smaller Topaz and, in 1972, the Sapphire.

Interior layout of the Amethyst was planned with balance in mind. On one side were the heavy appliances – cooker, fridge and sink – placed immediately adjacent to the door and over the centre-axle. On the other side were sizable wardrobes to retain stability. This radically innovative model also featured a floor that could be lowered to generate adequate headroom. Most importantly, however, was that the Amethyst was constructed using vacuum formed plastic panelling. This method of production was nothing new to Eccles who had already introduced plastic windows to

its range as well as to other brands within CI. The Amethyst concept came from the inventive mind of Tom Karren, who at the time was employed by David Ogle Ltd, Letchworth. This company had been started in 1954 creating stylish household electrical appliances but made a name for itself in the 1960s with various relatively successful studies in automobile design. Mainly utilising Riley and Mini floor pans, but later re-bodying Aston Martins and Daimlers, Ogle were probably best known for their involvement with the development of the Bond Bug, Reliant Robin and

replacement items not in stock or indeed obsolete could be fabricated from scratch before dispatching. Their commitment was to offer a 24-hour turn around for anything kept in stock and a maximum of three weeks if the piece needed to be specially made. In these cases, a number of identical parts would be produced to allow for the possibilities of future demand. CI had dealerships across the country and orders for replacement items were taken locally and sent through to the Suffolk headquarters.

Another subsidiary of CI was OBI Camping Ltd who were able to provide awnings to fit all models in the Fairholme, Eccles, Europa and Sprite family.

When Britain was plunged into another recession during the early-1980s, Alper's empire could not sustain the cost of production and, in 1982, CI went into receivership. Cosalt, the Grimsby based conglomerate whose divisional brands included the Humber Caravan Company and the old Pearman Briggs concern of Safari, bought the rights to all CI's ancillaries and in merging with their own assets became Cosalt International. In time, all interests in the manufacture of touring caravans would be sold again, and re-branded as Sterling Caravans, part of the Swift Group.

Reliant Scimitar GTE. With this kind of grounding, Ogle were well-placed to devise something special for Eccles. The Amethyst was launched at the 1969 Earls Court Show and represented quite a shift from normal caravan practice. Unfortunately, the buying public were not so enamoured with its unusual looks and by 1975, the Amethyst name was adorning a less remarkable design.

A lot of CI's success lay in a dependable after-sales department. Floor space of the Newmarket factory had been set aside for maintaining an off-the-shelf parts service with its own dedicated workshop. Any

Modern Times

Whilst CI were busily conquering the world, other rival manufacturers were quietly making a name for themselves and Humberside was one of a number of areas that developed as a centre for caravan production. Both Hull and Grimsby brought new names to the touring 'van market and Hull, especially, seemed to nurture a wealth of companies striving to outdo each other in the huge caravan trade that emerged during the 1960s.

During the preceding two decades, Humberside had already been identified as ideally placed for importing raw materials and exporting manufactured goods, and some of those firms established within easy reach of the docks at Kingston-upon-Hull significantly profited from European sales.

Around the same time as Henry and Sam Alper were founding Alperson Products in London, Walter Allen was looking to ease the post-War housing crisis to the north. Willerby Caravans was incorporated during mid-1944 and out-shopped mass-produced caravans of steel frames and canvas sides. By the 1950s and certainly into the 1960s, the company had a healthy following and sales were promising with popular models such as the Heatherbelle, Falcon, Jupiter and Vagabond. In 1961, 12 Willerby touring 'vans were shipped out to the deserts of Jordan and used

by the crew filming the Peter O'Toole epic, Lawrence of Arabia. Whilst this alone gave good exposure to the firm, a thriving overseas trade was developed through sales of the Willerby Dandy.

Astral Caravans of Stoneferry in the northern part of Hull were well known among Romany folk and prided themselves on building caravans aimed at the travelling entertainer. Indeed, there was a time when it was not unusual to find at least one example of an Astral on any show ground

countrywide. Names given to the models often reflected the Romany and showman interest such as Gaytime, Gypsy, Gypsylet, Varda (from the earliest form of covered 'vans), and Lavengro (after George Borrow's 1851 semi-autobiographical book, Lavengro: The Scholar, the Gypsy, the Priest). Astral's first showman's 'van was the Ranger launched in 1962 which was followed by the Luxitrailer and the Road Ranger, both fitted with toilet compartments and well appointed kitchen as standard.

Prior to producing the Ranger, Astral had offered the Travellyte to the touring market, subsequently joined by the relatively short-lived Cameo (although this model name was revived and enjoyed greater success towards the end of the 1970s). The Ranger inspired a series of touring 'vans of that name, and kept the company in pocket for more than a decade.

Whilst Bailey, who had been established in the west country during 1948 and were by now utilising standard off-the-shelf chassis made by B&B as the basis of construction, and the east coast firm of Carlight – with their Casetta, Cosmopolitan, Caribbean and Continental models – remained competitive brands, many names such as Castleton and Balmforth came and went as a fluctuating economic climate forced the smaller companies to close or be sold and swallowed into much larger concerns. Unfortunately, the 1960s foreign package holiday was emerging as a serious threat to caravan sales and with a period of fuel shortages affecting all motoring interests, the future of the industry looked decidedly bleak. Nevertheless, there were still a diehard band of travellers who yearned

to pursue a simpler way of life and sleeping under canvas was as popular as ever with the Camping Club of Great Britain & Ireland boasting 50,000 members (today the figure is ten times that number!).

It was from this period that many British manufacturers who form the mainstay of today's caravan industry were founded, either upon strong mergers or begun with solid business planning.

In 1965, Swift were set up at Cottingham in the East Riding of Yorkshire. Their aim was to build caravans of the highest quality that encompassed the most up-to-date

Above: This Romany four-berth was made by Castleton of Sherborne, Dorset in 1968. It is pictured in the classic caravan display at the Great Dorset Steam Fair.

Far Left: The 1962 Siddall Delta. Like the Eccles Amethyst, this caravan, modern-looking for the time, was designed by Tom Karren.

materials, technology and most essential and latest caravanning gadgetry. Swift soon attracted a loyal band of enthusiasts and the company steadily grew.

At the end of the 1960s, the world was enraptured by two pioneers, Buzz Aldrin and Neil Armstrong, taking the first human steps upon the moon. At about the same time, two other intrepid men, Brian Talbot and Ken Wilcock, were setting up a firm in Farington near Preston and, seizing upon the moment, started trading under the name Lunar. Having both previously worked as joiners for neighbouring manufacturer, Knowsley Caravans, the partnership were endeavouring to create a highest

Above: A 1996
ABI Award
Dawnstar.

quality lightweight touring van that could eventually vie within the very competitive luxury market.

In 1972, a new conglomerate was formed when the Hull-based Ace Caravan Company Ltd joined forces with static home manufacturer, Belmont Caravan Company Ltd to become Ace Belmont International. The mantle of constructing touring vans was placed in the hands of subsidiary firm, ABI Caravans Ltd. Their strength within the industry was enhanced a year later with the takeover of Elddis Caravans Ltd who had, since 1965, developed a solid reputation for quality but modestly priced caravans filling a niche hitherto not offered by the ABI range. This

was a shrewd move as high inflation considerably pushed up the cost of raw materials and the buying public were choosing to limit their spending. The Monza was announced in 1973 to rival Sam Alper's Sprite whilst the budget priced Prima range was Bailey's response and rival manufacturers soon followed suit.

In 1974, Lunar unveiled the Clubman range, an iconic design of the age that cemented the company's future within the industry. By this time the popularity of the firm's products had necessitated a move from Preston to larger premises in an old mill a few miles south of the Ribble.

The decade saw a larger number of mod cons included on standard spec sheets as the intrepid caravanner became ever more adventurous. British tourists were travelling further than ever before in pursuit of experiencing a diversity of cultures, and fast roads across Europe were enabling them to journey to new terrain with more unforgiving weather conditions. Caravan producers had to incorporate satisfactory insulation for colder conditions and adequate forms of internal air conditioning and food refrigeration for hotter climes.

At the start of the 1980s, the Lunar Delta range had also been introduced which catered for the lightweight caravan market.

With increasing holidaymakers being attracted to the pursuit of leisure caravanning, The Camping Club of Great Britain & Ireland changed its name to The Camping and Caravanning Club to encompass greater membership.

Bailey unveiled a sloping front to their caravans that for the first time enclosed the gas locker within the bodywork and below the seating of the front dinette. Up until then,

the locker had represented a rather unsightly protuberance added almost as an afterthought above the towing bracket and with Bailey's innovation finally stowing it neatly out of sight set the blueprint for future designs and imitators.

By the 1990s, the huge ABI factory was covering 21 acres and producing some of the most popular caravan ranges sold in Britain during the period. The Elddis brand had by then broken away to become an independent operator and with steady expansion and company buyouts would, by the end of the decade, represent part of the second

largest caravan manufacturing group.

As the new century dawned, Brian Talbot and Ken Wilcock decided to sell their assets in Lunar to a largely European conglomerate called the Tirus Group. It was a short-lived arrangement, however, and a 2007 management buyout ensured that Lunar would return to being a wholly British-built concern.

Today, there are hundreds of campsites that cater for the modern caravanner with dedicated hook-ups to provide electricity for lighting, the television, the fridge/freezer and the power shower. A stroll around the site will reveal one or two rarities, brands that have long since disappeared from the scene or caravans that are built in small production runs dotted among the various pitches, and of course a sprinkling of foreign 'invaders' to add to the interest. But one thing that becomes immediately noticeable is the great number of caravans represented by just a handful of brand names.

Elddis, had in the 1980s become part

Left: A Swift
Charisma basks
in the August sun
at the Camping &
Caravanning Club
site in Delamere
Forest.

of the Hull-based ABI Group, but were able to break away again and once more began developing their own independent identity. In the late-1990s, Elddis bought out Compass and Coachman to add to its other holdings of Crown and Herald. In so doing, the conglomerate became the Explorer Group, the second largest caravan producer behind Swift.

When Swift was started in the mid-1960s, little could the founders have known that by the end of the 20th Century, it would have given its name to one of the largest caravan manufacturing organisations in the world. In 1986, the firm entered the camper van market – a move which was to be the start of an extraordinary programme of expansion. With the financial prosperity yielded through Swift Caravans and Swift Motorhomes sales in the 1990s came the opportunity for the group to invest. Their standing within the Industry was gradually enhanced by the successive purchase of Abbey Caravans, Sprite Leisure (from Cosalt International which included the Safari, Eccles, Fairholme and Europa trading rights), and the bankrupt Bessacarr Caravans. The Bessacarr range was continued for another ten years but in an attempt to streamline manufacturing processes and rein in build costs, it was decided in 2007 to drop the name from caravan production. A substantial band of enthusiasts voiced their disappointment and so as not to let down their loyal customers, the management chose to continue a limited run that could only be bought through two dealerships based in Louth in Lincolnshire and Swindon, Wiltshire.

Today, the Swift Group also encompasses the assets and respective subsidiaries of Ace Caravans and Autocruise Motorhomes, and boasts Bessacarr Motorhomes, Ace Motorhomes, Swift Holiday Homes, Mondial Camper Vans and Escape Motorhomes under the huge Swift banner. In the mid-1990s, the Sprite brand was re-launched as Sterling Caravans and with the lion's share of the market, one would be hard-pressed to find a campsite during the season that does not contain at least several

examples of caravans and camper vans made by one or more concerns within the Swift Group.

Bailey who, throughout their 60-year history, have survived the ravishes of debilitating inflation, fuel shortages and national economic crisis, remains one of the longest standing and most popular producers within the industry with almost 10,000 caravans leaving their factory lines each year. In 1996, the Ranger – a name once used by both Alperson Products of Stratford and Astral Caravans of Stoneferry – was launched, immediately proving to be a best seller, and with the latest Orion, Olympus, Pegasus and Unicorn ranges utilising state-of-the-art Alu-Tech body shell construction, Bailey continue to be something of an industry trailblazer.

Alu-Tech is possibly the most significant development in the field of caravan technology in recent times and is worthy of further explanation here. Traditionally, each caravan was built up of many panels and held together with an inner framework. Ever since their conception, caravans, and especially the panelling that makes up the walls and roof, have been prone to distortion

Right & Far Right: Bailey's latest Alu-Tech system showing the way body and roof parts are bonded using interlocking aluminium extrusion instead of external fixing points.

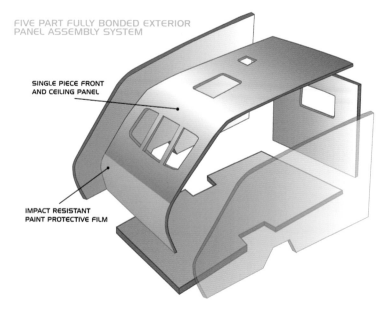

FIVE PART FULLY BONDED EXTERIOR PANEL ASSEMBLY SYSTEM

SINGLE PIECE FRONT AND CEILING PANEL

IMPACT RESISTANT PAINT PROTECTIVE FILM

from the effects of rain water seeping between external seams and fixings. The Alu-Tech system does away with 90% of these and, instead uses a minimal amount of aluminium outer framework simply designed to attach one panel to another at the edges, and held in place via hidden internal fixtures. There are five elements that make up the structural integrity to each 'van; a floor, two laminated sides,

a laminated rear panel, and a single piece that includes the roof and front panel, and extensive use of plastic throughout means there is no timber to warp or expand.

Bailey wanted to create an assembly technique that could revolutionise caravan production and did not skimp at any stage throughout development. The Department of Mechanical Engineering at the University of Bath

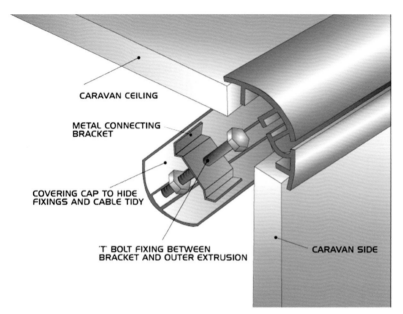

CARAVAN CEILING

METAL CONNECTING
BRACKET

COVERING CAP TO HIDE
FIXINGS AND CABLE TIDY

'T' BOLT FIXING BETWEEN
BRACKET AND OUTER EXTRUSION

CARAVAN SIDE

were asked to study the design for stress and weak points using state-of-the-art computer modelling, and a completed test vehicle was taken to the Millbrook Proving Ground in Bedfordshire and put through the rigours of a standard automotive durability test. This included seven days and more than 650 miles of gruelling trials over potholes, kerbs, adverse terrain to twist chassis and suspension, hills and high speed towing to examine effects on aerodynamics, simulating the sort of treatment a caravan might endure during a three-year period. The test vehicle was then subjected to extreme levels of temperature and humidity. Satisfied by the results, Bailey believe Alu-Tech is a huge step forward for the Industry and see it as a new direction in which other manufacturers are likely to follow.

Pulling A Fast One!

In 1932, the participants of the prestigious but gruelling Monte Carlo Rally included publicity manager of the Humber Hillman Group, Dudley Noble, with A. Clive Scarff of the Surrey-based Nomad Caravan dealership acting as co-driver. In tow behind their Hillman Wizard was an Eccles caravan, a most effective publicity stunt which proved that by finishing in a quite magnificent 35th place overall, an Eccles could be safely towed at great speeds.

Soon after, a Car Cruiser, again towed by a Hillman Wizard raced across the Sahara Desert covering 3,000 miles in just 21 days. Not to be outdone, Eccles repeated the exercise with a Humber Snipe and so began a regular succession of evermore demanding challenges, contested to gain maximum media exposure.

In 1951, it was the turn of Sam Alper to hit the headlines. An endurance run covering 4,400 miles had been organised by a French caravan magazine. Beginning in London, it visited Holland, Belgium, France, Germany, Switzerland and Italy, with the finishing line in Florence. The event was won by Alper towing a Sprite. Like the Rileys before him, Alper realised the value in this kind of publicity and a year later drove 10,000 miles around the Mediterranean in just 33 days,

again towing a Sprite. Throughout the 1960s, Sprites were put through the rigours of long-distance endurance tests over desert, mountain passes and uncharted territory. The 1964 Monte Carlo Rally even included an entry of a Ford Zephyr towing a Sprite Alpine which surprisingly was able to conquer most of the mountain stages without major incident.

In 1972, two caravans from the Sprite range were towed 1,000 miles over a 24 hour period around the racing circuit at Zandvoort, Holland, in an attempt to demonstrate the standards of safety to which these

models had been built, and to win over European customers. The following year, Alper drove a Mini 10,000 miles across the Sierra Nevada with a Sprite 400 in tow.

Within every motoring interest there has always developed a competitive element, be it timed trials, off-roading, circuit racing and so on, and so it was with the caravan fraternity. In the 1930s, regional Club meets would often include various events testing driver aptitude whilst towing a 'van. They were a chance to entertain fellow members and, although there were always going to be some spirited participants, these low-key tournaments were never regarded as anything more than a sideshow to the actual Club get-together.

In 1954, a new craze emerged – Road Rallying. To the spectators, this might have seemed an interesting and often spectacular alternative to car racing but was viewed by the caravan industry very much as a serious proving ground for their products and, more importantly, a demonstration of endurance against safety and stability under the watchful eye of the buying public. The competition was divided into several categories that would rigorously scrutinize and evaluate all issues associated with towing a caravan such as reversing, braking and speed trials. Tentatively advertised, The Caravan Club British Caravan Road Rally of 1954 nevertheless attracted enormous enthusiasm and application to enter was over-subscribed right from the off.

Participants in the early days would typically drive to the event and all being well would, after the contest and

Below: Road Rallying was a perfect way for manufacturers to demonstrate to the public the stability, manoeuvrability, safety and other qualities in their products. Here, the teams of Bessacarr, Lynton and Eccles line up during one event. Behind the Ford Granada is an Eccles Amethyst, at the time a radical new approach to caravan design.

Right: A caravan race in action. Things didn't always go this smoothly though.

award ceremony, drive home again, hopefully with their caravan still intact and preferably devoid of scrapes and dents!

By the 1960s, Road Rallying, far from regarded as a novelty sport, was attracting professionally managed works' teams from the industry's manufacturers and with decent sponsorship and prize money on offer, was also seducing world-famous motor racing drivers to try their hand at putting a car and caravan outfit through its paces. Inevitably, racing speeds began to increase and the number of privateers not having a company's financial backing began to dwindle.

As the 1970s dawned, even the Establishment were starting to lose interest as the costs of preparing a racing outfit as well as supplying spares and a dedicated support crew were severely eating into precious budgets. By the middle of the decade it was clear that Road Rallying was on its way out and in 1976, after 22 years of pitting driver skill and caravan durability against the clock, The Caravan Club held its last competitive meeting.

The Expand and Collapse

Slide out extensions are commonplace on some of today's largest motor homes but it was way back in the 1920s that the idea first materialised. Alfred Ensor was an early proponent and his collapsible-type trailers could be expanded to form larger than the average living accommodation. Later, he developed the Ensor Wrekin, a rigid tourer designed in the mid-1930s that incorporated an additional fold-out space for cooking.

Fairway of Llandudno used a similar extension to conveniently position a lavatory cubicle.

Another firm that saw potential in a folding annexe for toilet facilities was Bampton. Reg and Ted Bampton were vehicle coachbuilders but left the motor trade in 1932 and set up business in Swindon specialising in expanding caravans. Their first foray produced the unusual little Easitow, a 'van measuring only 10ft x 4ft 9in that had a side panel hinged along the top edge and a sliding section that, together, added another 3ft 6in to the width, enough room for a decent size double bed converted from the sofa. The Bamptons found construction of 'expandables' very time-consuming and after turning their attention to the war effort in the 1940s, did not resume building the type thereafter.

The design of the post-War Dinky Rambler must have taken much inspiration from the likes of the Easitow and continued the practice of adding full

length bed space transversely across the width of the 'van. Weighing just 241kg, the Rambler found favour among owners of higher-powered motorcycle and sidecar combinations which, for many, proved an extremely cheap form of holidaying.

Where most caravan annexes extended outwards from the sides, the 1954 Gilderex by Northampton Caravan Ltd gained extra space from the front over the towing hitch making an already large 21ft towable 'van into a 27ft long mansion! Similarly, the Berkeley Governor could be extended at the back from 22ft to 27ft with a quadrant shaped annexe hinged on the rear chassis member.

Another firm, Spacetrekker announced the 520 in the late 1970s. On the surface it looked very much like any other 'van of the period but cleverly incorporated a section of elevating roof with 'first floor' accommodation for another two occupants.

The Sprite Compact was unveiled in 1981 and for a caravan possessing a 12ft x 6ft 8in body, tipped the scales at an impressive 685kg. In an attempt at reducing weight and increasing aerodynamics, it was designed with a very low profile but to allow for full standing room, it too featured an elevating roof but this time stretching the entire length of the 'van. At 4ft 5in, the entrance door was not much bigger that that of a car's and, after a brief existence, lack of sales forced Sprite to drop the Compact from their

HERE IT IS—

THE NEW THREE-WHEEL ENSOR

BUILT ON AN ENTIRELY NEW KIND OF CHASSIS

AT LAST——PERFECTLY STEADY TOWING AT ALL SPEEDS

Another feature exclusive to Ensors

The FOLDING KITCHEN

leaving you ever so much more space in the caravan itself

15 feet 4-berth

£160

Folding Kitchen £10 extra.

*A catalogue giving full details of this remarkable caravan is now ready. Send a postcard for your copy.

C. A. ENSOR

Ketley :: Wellington :: Salop

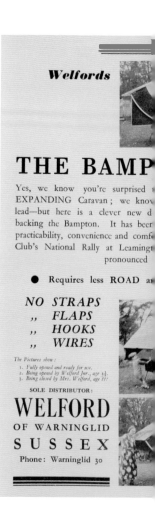

Welfords

THE BAMP[TON]

Yes, we know you're surprised [at this] EXPANDING Caravan; we know[...] lead—but here is a clever new d[esign] backing the Bampton. It has been [...] practicability, convenience and comf[ort...] Club's National Rally at Leaming[ton...] pronounced [...]

● Requires less ROAD a[nd...]

NO STRAPS
,, FLAPS
,, HOOKS
,, WIRES

The Pictures show:
1. Fully opened and ready for use.
2. Being opened by Welford Jnr., age 3½.
3. Being closed by Mrs. Welford, age 7½.

SOLE DISTRIBUTOR:

WELFORD

OF WARNINGLID

SUSSEX

Phone: Warninglid 30

catalogue.

Whilst many manufacturers looked for ways of adding space to conventional rigid 'vans once pitched on the campsite, others concentrated their efforts on creating collapsible caravans that could surreptitiously be squirreled away between uses.

The encouraging sales Eccles, Hutchings and other manufacturers experienced after the end of World I caught the attention of established tent makers, Piggott Brothers of London who soon announced their own touring 'van. Taking advantage of their expertise in making canvas marquees, Piggott launched

Below: The Ensor Wrekin of 1947.

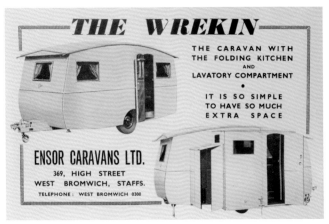

Above: A larger version of the Bampton announced in 1938.

Centre: This Berkeley demonstrates the novel ways manufacturers attempted to add space to caravans that were already of maximum manageable length for towing!

a series of collapsible trailers appealing to many for the ease in which they could be dismantled and conveniently stored during the low season or between tours. The Piggott range were characterised by canvas panelling stretched and laced over a wooden frame and ingeniously incorporated such features as bay windows, a lantern roof, storage cupboards and, on some models, even a stow-away veranda.

To avoid losing sales and to compete with an ever increasing choice of motor caravan, Eccles also offered a collapsible option on all their standard range and in time this sector of the market was joined by other brands.

Shadow, a firm hailing from Wolverhampton, and ATC of Maidstone both produced rigid 'collapsibles' of a similar design to each other, where the top half could be neatly lowered down via a winding mechanism to envelop the bottom half. This had the advantage that none of the windows or indeed the interior fittings such as kitchen units, sofa-beds and any stowed luggage or equipment were compromised when the 'van was collapsed. Storage, especially in the top half was naturally lost, however, and when in transit, the close proximity of the windows to the road meant that they would often be prone to damage from

loose stone chippings. One solution to this was the folding caravan whereby the top half comprising the windows could concertina, bringing the roof down flat on top of the bottom half like a lid, and completely protecting the windows inside the closed trailer.

The Walpole was an entirely different take on the 'collapsible' caravan as it was made up of rigid sections that could be fully dismantled and flat-packed when stored between uses. This meant that before leaving home, the sides and roof needed to be assembled so that in transit, it looked like a purpose-built tourer.

Having built a reputation for elegant tourers, the Coventry firm, Airlite, tried their hand at 'collapsibles' with the Minx. This was a supremely compact vehicle measuring just 10ft 6in in length and less than 6ft in height but boasting a very eye-catching teardrop profile and, as with all Airlites, their signature Art-Deco style sunrise side windows. It was unveiled in 1937, the year the firm started fitting Bottogas cooking equipment as standard and also the last year of Airlite caravan production. Among other makes of the 'collapsible' before World War II were Fohlo and Foldavan.

Available from 1960 was the Portafold (later Ansfold), a state-of-the-art collapsible 'van that took much inspiration from the

Right: The Fohlo Caravan was popular due to it's collapsible nature.

Far Right: One of the most popular folding caravans was the Foldavan. It was built in Emsworth, Hampshire for over a decade.

The **FOHLO** CARAVAN

The CARAVAN that has a FULLY OPENING ROOF

A PLEASURE TO TOW—NOT A WORRY

READY FOR THE ROAD	READY FOR USE
3ft. 7ins. HIGH 4ft. WIDE	7ft. 2ins. HIGH 7ft. WIDE 6ft. 2ins. HEAD ROOM
EASY TOWING NO EXTRA WIND RESISTANCE	SEATS SIX
TUCKS IN BEHIND THE SMALLEST CAR ON THE ROAD	SLEEPS 2 ADULTS AND 2 CHILDREN Price £125

W. S. GREENING, 240c, Clapham Road, Stockwell, London, S.W.9

1950s Fairholme Wanderer. The Portafold was built in Emsworth, Hampshire by Portaplas Ltd and utilised glass reinforced plastic (GRP) for much of the construction. Modestly advertised as "The Finest Folding Caravan in the World" and "The Caravan of the Future... Today!", it was jovially endorsed in the marketing campaign as "a marvellous piece of workmanship" by none other than Dr Who actor, Jon Pertwee! Designed to enable assembly by just one person, the vehicle consisted of a trailer base,

four separate sides hinged to the base, and a trailer lid that doubled as the roof. Each side had a centrally placed handle for ease of assembly and a split rear entrance door gave access to the accommodation – a three-way bench seat that could be converted to either three single beds and a bunk, or two double beds where the occupants slept side by side in a line, like sardines! Despite its cosy interior, the Portafold gained a popular following and production continued right up to the early 1980s.

The Minnows

The 1920s and '30s saw a race emerge between British motor manufacturers, especially Austin, Ford and Morris, to build a small car that could adequately convey a typically sized family but most importantly be affordable to the masses. Austin unveiled their Seven, Morris launched the Minor and, in 1932, Ford joined the fray with their Model Y, the first full four-seater saloon priced new at just £100. In response to this growing trend, compact and lightweight caravans were made available and with space gained via the addition of an awning, these too became very popular.

The Hammersmith-based firm, Raven, marketed the diminutive two-berth Argonette which, at only 9ft in length and weighing just 5½cwt was one of the smallest rigid caravans ever manufactured in England. Argonettes were for a short while another model that attracted good sales among owners of motorcycle and sidecar combinations. Not to be outdone, Rudge Whitworth, Coventry motorcycle manufacturers since 1911, provided their own version, marketed from 1927.

Not content with towing a caravan behind a sidecar outfit, Edward Bowser of Leeds invented a two-berth accommodation unit that could be unfolded from the actual sidecar itself!

Around 1930, the Scottish firm of Thomson unveiled their first in a series of compacts, a most unusual and more or less egg-shaped caravan but with a full-size door occupying half of the nearside side panel! Such was the lightness of construction that one owner managed to complete a 1,000 mile tour with a Morris Minor as tow-car, and reportedly used only 22 gallons of petrol at a cost of one (old) pence per mile!

After World War II, the tradition of providing a lightweight option continued and some companies specialised in and sometimes devoted all their attention to building caravans suitable for small family cars.

One of the post-War models was the Safari Minor, a caravan of roughly cuboid dimensions that, thanks to a clever use of the limited space available, was surprisingly well-appointed for a 'van so small. Conceived by the firm of

Above:
When motor manufacturers began building small cars like the Austin 7 in an attempt to get more people of lesser means on the road, caravan companies responded and a market for micro-caravans rapidly developed.

Pearman Briggs, it was built without using a conventional chassis and relied on the floor mounted storage units for rigidity. The Minor's distinguishing feature was a double door entrance positioned over the towing hitch at the front, an attempt to create the illusion of greater capacity, and although the Minor was only designed as a two-berth, an optional matching awning was available allowing extra sleeping accommodation. A dinette at the rear doubled as a bed, whilst large cupboards either side of the doorway concealed storage space as well as a twin-burner gas stove and fold-away sink. Safari later went on to make tourers aimed at the luxury market and in 1968 were taken over by Cosalt of Grimsby, eventually becoming just one part that made up the huge Swift Group.

The Paladin Pixy was announced in 1952 and represented one of the smallest four-berth caravans ever to grace the caravan market. Panelled with hardboard and measuring just 8ft 6in x 6ft 2in, holidaying in a Pixy must have been an intimate affair where friendships were either thoroughly bonded or, quite likely, lost forever!

A year later, Car Trailers Ltd of Harpenden introduced the Zephyr, a caravan that had a largely circular side

elevation and designed to accommodate two adults and a child at a squeeze. Its shape offered good headroom as well as structural integrity and appeared well equipped with gas powered cooking stove, cheerfully coloured upholstery and a snazzy "cigarette-proof" plastic table fitted as standard! The mighty Ford Motor Company, however, was a little perturbed by the model's name and Car Trailers Ltd hastily changed it

from Zephyr to the Countess Minor!

In Dundee, R. Stewart and Sons were manufacturing the Nutshell. Possessing little more length and breadth than a Mini, this ludicrously small caravan was snug for one, lascivious for two and would have been considered record breaking for

Above: An Advertisement for the 1934 Atlas Two.

Below: A Standard Eight and Car Trailers Ltd Countess Minor, here pictured at St. Ives in Cornwall.

any more. Built throughout the 1950s, it weighed just 2cwt and could be bought for just £98.

The Willerby Tip-Top, at just 9ft long, was advertised as "the link between camping adventure and caravan luxury". It had sleeping accommodation for three and was of such lightweight construction that, like the Nutshell, was aimed towards owners of cars in the Mini, Hillman Imp and Renault Dauphine class.

Sam Alper, ever the entrepreneur and keen to increase sales, launched

the Sprite Aerial in the late-1950s and in so doing entered into the small caravan market. The Aerial's success went beyond expectation and when it was eventually replaced by the '400', orders shot through the roof. Such was the demand for the 400 (the name referring to its weight in kilograms), that it remained in production right through to the mid-1970s.

Today, the compact caravan market is still a thriving business and one of the mainstays is Eriba, a company started by Eric Bachem over 50

years ago. Bachem, an aeronautics engineer, was determined to adapt his knowledge and skills to the production of lightweight and very rigid caravans and designed a revolutionary tubular steel frame skeleton inside of which the body panels and interior furniture were attached. The walls were made with polyurethane foam insulation affording minimal temperature variations and a saving on heating costs. Like the 1970s Spacetrekker 520 and the 1980s Sprite Compact, the Eriba was made available with elevating roof to add standing room – a concept that, for this company at least, has stood the test of time. Eriba are now owned by specialist camper van manufacturers Hymer who seem committed to continuing production, whilst a healthy enthusiasm for these distinctive little 'vans is actively maintained by the Eriba Owners Club of Great Britain.

At the time of writing, two of the newest brands to enter the 'micro' industry are The English Caravan Company, and Pod Caravans Limited of Taunton.

Founded in Hertfordshire by Richard Stark, The English Caravan Company

Left: Eric Bachem started caravan manufacture in the late-1950s with a distinctive range of aeronautically inspired designs. Pictured is one of the diminutive but very popular Pucks featuring the pop-top roof that Bachem continued to develop for the Eriba series.

Left: The Eriba still represents one of the smallest, most lightweight and compact micro caravans on the market that can easily be towed by lower powered cars. This example, pictured on a site in St. Malo, dates from 1991.

Right & Far Right: The Hertfordshire-based English Caravan Company is one of several modern day manufacturers looking to emulate the designs of yesteryear, but taking advantage of state-of-the-art technology and build materials. Here is the beautifully finished Classic Teardrop.

aims to combine modern build materials with retro styling whilst all vehicles are lovingly hand-built and benefit from great attention to period detailing. The diminutive two-berth Tilly harks back to teardrop streamlining of a previous age providing up-to-date yet appropriately styled caravans not only for owners of post-War classic vehicles, but for those who appreciate something just that little bit more quirky!

Likewise, the Pod is also teardrop shaped and at around just over 10½ft long (including the towing hitch) and weighing in at between 250kg and 350kg, represents one of the smallest 'vans on the modern caravan market. Again its graceful lines emulate the designs of the inter-war years and with such modest dimensions and chic personality, would suit a small American classic and, equally, not look out of place behind either a first generation or latest version Fiat 500.

Presenting Those Who Dared to be Different!

Probably the most unconventional company in the history of caravan manufacture was Coventry Steel. After the collapse of Airlite in 1938, Clifford Dawltrey joined forces with component makers Rubery Owen to build smooth seamless caravans made initially of rolled steel, and later of weight-saving aluminium. The body of the first model, the Phantom Knight, displayed not a single straight line but distinctly borrowed styling cues from the flat-sided Airlite range. When production resumed after the War, Dawltrey pushed his innovative skills to the limit with the Falstaff Knight, Silver Knight and Warwick Knight. Using narrow and formed aluminium strips interlocked vertically, insulated with

Onazote (an expanded synthetic rubber material with outstanding heat retaining characteristics), and lined with a layer of polished oak veneer for the interior, they represented caravans the like of which had never been seen before. Inside it was no less inspired, the Falstaff Knight for example containing carpeted staircases to each of the separately partitioned single beds at the rear and a double bed at the front. Below the sleeping accommodation the floor stepped down to avoid excessive loss of headroom and provided two areas, one for seating and one for dining. Beyond the dining area was a bathroom complete with full-size bath and sink. A large central room above the axle benefited from full standing

height and consisted of kitchen and cloakroom with optional flush chemical toilet. With entrance gained through a stable-type split door, the Knights were strikingly unorthodox but sumptuously comfortable vehicles. They also had a price tag to match and were not huge sellers.

During the mid-1950s, Dawltrey once again surprised the caravan fraternity with the Kampa Knight, a strange corrugated plywood box with upper side panels made up entirely of louvered vents and, at the front, windows on a 'V' shaped panel. With the company concentrating more and more on commercial and utility trailer construction, this was to be the last of Dawltrey's designs before he left the business altogether.

As glass-reinforced plastic (GRP) became the experimental caravan manufacturing material of the 1950s, whole new possibilities opened up as GRP could be moulded to practically

"COVENTRY KNIGHT 47"

AS MODERN AS TOMORROW'S NEWS!

In Steady Production for Home and Overseas

STANDARD MODEL £1,650 COMPLETE

COVENTRY STEEL CARAVANS LTD.

Exchange Works   *Warwick*

Reg. Design 845558/9, 848804. Pat. No. 568680. Other patents pending

Above: A Coventry Knight advertisement from 1947 showing the unusual lines typical of Clifford Dawltrey's many design ideas.

any shape. It proved extremely strong, was not prone to the level of rotting suffered by vehicles made of wood or wood-based products, and the caravan's final livery could be applied at the moulding stage by infusing colour with the gel-coat.

Charles Panter was an early advocate of caravans made of GRP with some interesting designs emerging from his Biggleswade factory – the Berkeley displaying some of the styling touches more associated with the motor industry. Panter, however, had ambitions to produce a small sports car using similar construction techniques and collaborated with Lawrence Bond to build a car to rival the Austin-Healey Sprite. With recession hitting the caravan industry in the early-1960s, development costs could not be sustained and the company filed for bankruptcy.

Revolutionary vehicles such as Willerby's Vista, featuring a wide wrap of windows at the front, and the futuristic Vogue had entered the fray and although GRP was for the time being judged too heavy, the radical styling achieved from its use would influence generations of caravan designs to come.

Yet there were those who tried to be different in a less positive way.

In the mid-1950s, Rollalong were an established firm based in Ringwood, Hampshire, having moved from Cheltenham after the War. The company gained notability in 1955 when The Caravan Club commissioned them to construct a miniature caravan measuring just 6ft 9in in length, which was subsequently presented to the royal household for Prince Charles and Princess Anne to play in.

In 1936, however, Roll-Along (as

they were then known) really broke the mould and unveiled the Streamer to an unprepared public. It is fair to say that the Streamer was not the company's greatest idea as it tried very hard to be too many things and ended up portraying something of a nasty accident between a tourer and a conventional box caravan. The front half ahead of the axle was not unlike the style of the 1950s and could possibly have been a peek into the future, whilst the rear half represented a startling glance into Dr Frankenstein's laboratory! A narrow lantern roof grafted onto the full-width frontal aspect extended horizontally straight out the back, ending squarely and abruptly above a double door entrance, and flanked on either side by the roof line shoulders usually found on a streamlined tourer. This gave it the appearance not unlike a World War I tank! Well appointed with shower, bath and ample living area, it was placed on the market for the princely sum on £325, a high price in those days and due to its appearance, could not have been terribly popular. The bath, incidentally, was cleverly sunken into the floor and in the 1930s a number of manufacturers took advantage of this largely overlooked space for a variety

Below: A small lightweight sportscar might be an unusual subject to include in a book about caravans, but it was the production of the motorcycle-engined Berkeley which would eventually spell the end for the Biggleswade-based company that, until 1961, had successfully built quality caravans.

of uses. As long as there was sufficient ground clearance below the 'van, security lockers, extra storage units and trap doors for expelling unwanted dust and dirt were all incorporated between the chassis framework and, like Roll-Along's Streamer, all proved to be short-lived exercises!

Another company that had commenced construction in the south of England was Country Life, their first 'vans being built in Slough. Before

the War, Country Life caravans were not especially remarkable, being well-made contemporary styled vehicles incorporating a pleasing level of mod cons. When operations moved to Romsey in Hampshire, however, things started to go a little awry. Initial post-War designs were fairly promising and included the Languard, announced in 1947, providing the sort of interior space expected from a static home, yet retaining a neat and

Below: A small lightweight sportscar might be an unusual subject to include in a book about caravans, but it was the production of the motorcycle-engined Berkeley which would eventually spell the end for the Biggleswade-based company that, until 1961, had successfully built quality caravans.

attractive appearance. But when a fellow competitor introduced a two-storey caravan in 1951, Country Life decided to jump on the band wagon with the 22ft Lancraft. This was predominantly a standard-looking 'van monstrously disfigured by an unsightly growth that consisted of the top half of a smaller caravan manifesting from the Lancraft's roof and containing two upstairs bedrooms. It was not well-received and after disappointing sales, was understandably dropped from the Country Life catalogue.

And then there was the 17ft Moorland, a caravan for those with a penchant for the absolute ridiculous! Constructed on a four-wheel chassis, it outwardly represented a half-timbered cottage complete with dormer-style protrusions from the sloping pitched roof as well as a mock brick chimney to vent smoke from

the coal stove. Not surprisingly, sales were again decidedly poor.

Whilst the performance of new cars steadily improved, so did the nature of road development with straighter and safer high speed links. Britain's national speed limit was gradually raised and by the mid-1960s it had reached 70mph. The limit for towing a caravan or trailer, even on motorways, remained at a painfully slow 40mph. With the first section of the M6, the Preston Bypass, having opened in 1958, the restrictions increasingly caused other drivers to view caravanners as an encumbrance on the road and it is little wonder, therefore, that poorly designed models encouraged derisive comment from the critics.

The ugly Bluebird Joie de Vivre did little to help the cause with only cursory decoration to the exterior in the form of an alternately-coloured waist stripe. Jutting out above the towing hitch was a Luton-style overhang containing sleeping accommodation apparently inspired by American practice. With its severe lack of aesthetics, it is hard to comprehend how anyone was daft enough to buy one! Beauty, as they say, is in the eye of the beholder, however, and Astral of Hull included a Luton-style in their range too. The Joie de Vivre (meaning 'Joy of Living') fortunately did not enjoy a particularly long life and very few are known to exist today.

In the 1960s, even Sam Alper of CI fame dabbled with the unconventional

when, at The International Caravan Show, Earls Court, he unveiled a hovercraft Sprite to a bewildered public!

And then there were those rare occasions when caravanners, tired of the open road, could be found shoving their beloved 'vans in rivers and canals! This was not in any way a last desperate resort to rid themselves of their holiday frustrations but another concept that, over the history of leisure caravanning, has captured the imagination of several manufacturers – the amphibious caravan.

Representing little more than a shrunken houseboat on a demountable chassis, the Otter for example was one such venture and attempted to combine the pleasure of open road touring with the tranquillity of navigating Britain's waterways. Essentially a flat-bottom vessel, it was provided at the rear with an outboard motor and a narrow deck from where the 'captain' could take charge.

Raven was another firm to experiment with the 'amphibian' and aptly named their 1950 effort, the Duck, whilst Creighton made the Gull!

The problem seemed to be that there were insufficient caravanners who wished to own a water-borne vessel and, likewise, not many boat owners with the desire to holiday on the open road. Even fewer individuals wanted to combine the two modes of transport into one contraption and as a result, sales were inevitably poor.

In recent times, there have still

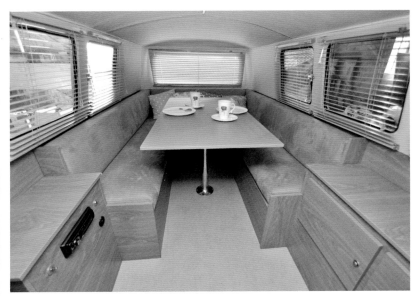

Left & Far Left:
Launched in 2010, the design of the Dub-box unashamedly takes inspiration from the Volkswagen split screen van of the 1950s, with retro-styling applied to the interior detailing as well. In 2011, it won The Caravan Club Lightweight Leisure Trailer Award for caravans of 750kg and under.

emerged some unusual takes on the caravan concept and in 2010, Dub-box of Herefordshire announced a distinctive new tourer styled on the 1950s Volkswagen Type 2, more commonly known as the 'split-screen van' or 'splitty'. The body for this two-berth centre-axle vehicle was entirely made of GRP and like some of the Eriba range described in the previous chapter, was available with an elevating roof. In 2011, the Dub-box, complete with two-ring gas stove,

stainless steel sink and an MP3 player could be purchased for around £14,000.

Another firm to take inspiration from an earlier age are the English Caravan Company already mentioned in the previous chapter. At the time of writing, their range consisted of three teardrop shaped models; the largest of these, named the 'Classic', evidently but refreshingly embracing Art Deco design cues from the likes of Clifford Dawltrey's pre-War Airlite range.

Bits and Bobs

Like all pastimes that arouse and consume the interests of active participants, caravanners have over the years come to use and rely on a huge range of accessories to enhance their holiday enjoyment. As well as providing extensive information to its members and assuring a level of standards at many associated sites, The Caravan Club has an archive dedicated to the collation, documentation and preservation of artefacts, ephemera and written accounts.

In 2007, the Club celebrated the centenary of its inauguration as The Caravan Club of Great Britain and Ireland, founded by 11 enthusiasts at the London home of fellow caravanner, J. Harris Stone. At the turn of the 21st Century, household membership had swelled to well over 250,000 and many long-standing subscribers were encouraged to contribute any period items, from the historically important to the simplest and mundanely practical, to tell their particular caravanning stories, help chronicle the development of the leisure caravan industry, and chart 100 years of The Caravan Club.

In addition to the Club's own records, the Collection Officer, Angela Cox, received a diversity of items such as regional and national commemorative pennants, badges, diaries, cine film and personal holiday photographs. With

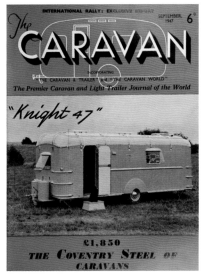

the origins of leisure caravanning stemming as far back as Dr William Gordon Stables first forays in 1885, many of the artefacts were extremely old and delicate, and understandably required specialist handling and storage to ensure their preservation for future generations. Indeed, two of the items were Stables' own business card detailing his profession as an author and includes an illustration of The Wanderer caravan, and a leather bound book dating from 1890 and entitled

Visitors, listing the many people Stables met on his travels.

The eclectic mix of ephemera shows that in those early years, the Club was very much a more intimate affair with annual dinner dance menus and membership lists for those few who were privileged enough to own a caravan.

Instruction manuals for individual models, AA membership cards, holiday destination information, The Caravan Club National Caravan Rally official programmes and adverts for the latest gadget have all helped to explain the social side of caravanning before, between and after the two World Wars. Of course there are programmes for most of the sixteen years companies and spirited individuals competed the sport of Road Rallying as well as regulations, insurance forms, a swathe of entry numbers and even a British Railways weigh bridge ticket – a requirement for the competition to ensure one's caravan was within the regulated specification.

The Caravan, En Route, and other magazines with caravan related articles plus sales catalogues and brochures are well represented as well as letters from some of the better known personalities within the Club fraternity.

The style of graphics and illustrations typify the era in which each piece of ephemera was printed and is in itself a fair record of contemporary design, dated in no small part by the caravans and tow-cars depicted in accompanying photographs. Postcards and officially commissioned Club Christmas cards all go to making the archive a useful source of research and education.

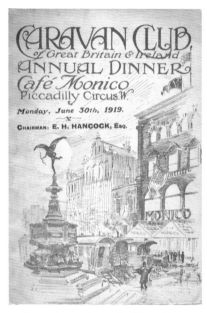

Several copies of The Caravan Song were taken into the Collection representing one of the more quirky items associated with the hobby. It was written by J. Harris Stone soon after the Club was formed and champions the tranquil life of the caravanner and the call of the open road away from "the mirth and moil of town". The music was composed by Dorothy Grierson, a fellow caravanner, who at meetings would rally the troops with a rip-roaring rendition. The actual tune, unfortunately, has to date remained lost in the annals of time.

Accessories are represented in the form of ceramics, crockery, glassware, tea sets, tablecloths, mugs, ashtrays and the odd thermos flask although the Collecting Policy for the Archive limits the type and size of object accepted into the Collection.

There is a colourful assortment of anniversary and rally pennants and banners that members would collect

and display from the windows of their 'vans, showing an array of fanciful area logos that almost always included the signature horseshoe motif of The Caravan Club.

Trophies, shields and tankards were regularly awarded at meetings and a large number have found their way into the Collection. Plaques, tie pins, lapel badges and Road Rally Marshal's badges are just some of the smaller items that might outwardly seem less significant that if it had not been for the setting up of the Archive, might have been disposed of and forgotten about completely.

A number of personal records and albums have been donated including the exploits of Ralph Lee, one of the longest serving members of both The Caravan Club and The Camping & Caravanning Club.

Above: A Caravan Club of Great Britain & Ireland pennant issued to members around 1908.

Left: Copies of the *Caravan Club Prospectus* issued during the 1930s show the diverse range of objects collected, documented and preserved by the Caravan Club Archive at Beaulieu.

The Adventures of Ralph and Muriel

The engaging hobby of caravanning has, for the majority of devotees, provided a relatively cheap means by which to escape the routine of everyday commitments or a chance to simply experience a change of scenery. For some, however, it has come to represent an all-consuming pastime and from time to time there are those individuals who demonstrate great adventure in their caravanning achievements. One such enthusiast was Ralph Lee, a seemingly unassuming person who became one of the most well-known and certainly well-travelled amongst the leisure caravan fraternity.

Born in Kettering in 1903, Lee developed a passion for camping at an early age and fabricated his own tent with the help of his mother's sewing machine. His father, recognising and encouraging his son's growing interest, gave Ralph an 18th birthday present of membership to what was in those days called The Camping Club. Later, the Club was renamed The Camping & Caravanning Club to encompass a wider patronage. Lee made good use of his home-made tent and formed healthy friendships with fellow campers including the architect of the Scout movement and, later, President of The Camping Club, Robert Baden-Powell.

On one such holiday, Ralph made the acquaintance of Muriel Waters and romance blossomed. In 1930, the couple married and spent their honeymoon camping in South Wales. It might have been the perfect

getaway had it not been for the appalling weather and, somewhat disconsolate, the newlyweds conceded it was time to upgrade to more comfortable accommodation for future trips. By then, the up-and-coming pastime attracting notable coverage in the motoring press was caravanning and the Lees decided this was an ideal opportunity to build their own 'van. Neither Ralph nor Muriel had the slightest idea what a two-wheeled caravan ought to look like but, like the early caravan manufacturers, took inspiration from horse-drawn four-wheeled 'gypsy'-type 'vans. Although the build resulted in a rather heavy vehicle, it was a vast improvement on the comparatively fragile and unreliable tent, and despite its weight issues could satisfactorily be pulled behind the couple's Singer Eight.

Thoughts had turned to how such a 'van should be attached to the rear of the car, but as this was uncharted territory, the Lees opted to simply bolt the two vehicles together via a pivot point! It was customary, however, for owners to give identity to their caravans and the Lees christened their new creation Who Cares after a popular song of the time.

The naivety by which their 'van had been conceived was soon realised and not

long after a second was laid out on the drawing board with much consideration to reducing overall weight. This was one of three further 'vans constructed between the wars, all sharing the same sturdy chassis utilising as a basis an axle from a Morris Cowley. Side panels were of plywood over a wooden frame, sleeping accommodation consisted of twin beds, and an unusual measure was to include a built-in lavatory – a feature still almost unheard of at the time.

The Lees' fifth caravan, appropriately named Who Cars V, was something of a diversion from previous practice – the first 'van purchased from an established manufacturer. The year was 1939, the family had grown with the arrival of daughter Patricia and with heightened concerns as to the likelihood of war in Europe, Ralph chose to relocate their 'van to a field near Guildford, a safe distance from their house

in the London district of Surbiton. This proved an incisive move as in 1942, the Lees suffered at the hands of the Luftwaffe, losing their home and most belongings during a night time bombing raid. Thankfully, the family were all safe and because of Ralph and Muriel's foresight, could take up residence in Who Cares V in Guildford,

the caravan becoming their home for the remainder of the War. To cope with the long winter months and improve living conditions, a coal stove was installed.

Although Ralph had been called up for active service with the Royal Air Force, his skills as a civilian dental surgeon were considered just as important and instead of taking the posting, he was allowed to continue practicing for the duration of the conflicts. Had it not been for his dedication to the dental profession, Ralph might well have succeeded as a caravan manufacturer, especially with the interest shown in his pre-War designs. Indeed, some of his ideas were inspirational to a number of those who had entered the caravan industry, including long-time friend, Sam Alper.

In 1947, Ralph joined the Caravan Club and his unwavering support to the pursuit of leisure caravanning did not go unnoticed. He and his 'van were invited to join the street procession as part of the annual Lord Mayors Parade, London, an occasion he often proclaimed was his most proudest, yet surreal!

With the declaration of peace came renewed motivation to travel and venture

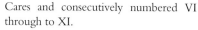

Below: Ralph and Muriel Lee became the first British Caravanners to cross the Arctic Circle in 1960.

further afield. 1947 certainly proved an exciting year for the Lees who took their post-War overseas vacation in Holland, a country still recovering from the aftermath of German occupation and Allied liberation. When the family sailed across the English Channel, it was one of 74 such crossings and the beginning of a love affair with the diversity in European culture. Over the next five decades, the Lees visited practically every country in Europe and Scandinavia, and always faithfully accompanied by one of six successive caravans, each christened Who

Cares and consecutively numbered VI through to XI.

The Lees' favourite destination was Greece, but the Alps, the Black Forest, and even a jaunt to Venice all proved little obstacle for the family who had become seasoned travellers. On one trip to France, after bedding down for the night in a deserted town square, they were awoken the next morning to find themselves completely surrounded by a bustling market!

On another tour, whilst crossing a river in Portugal, they were asked to draw back all their caravan's curtains as the 'van was blocking the captain's view from the ship's bridge and he could not see where he was going!

In 1960, they achieved fame by becoming the first British caravanners to cross the Arctic Circle and in so doing founded the Blue Nose Club! Soon after, they broke convention by securing permission to legally enter the Soviet Union without an officially appointed Russian chaperone.

In the post-War years, the Lees established a loyal following to the Gloucestershire firm, Cheltenham. This was a very successful manufacturer established by Arthur and Joy Gardener after having initially constructed a motor

caravan from an ex-army ambulance way back in 1919. Like Ralph's first efforts, Arthur Gardener had built this vehicle without much thought to either detail practicalities or fuel consumption and before long he designing his next creation – a centre-axle trailer type 'van. This was much more successful and prompted him to enter serious production.

After World War II, a friendship blossomed between the Gardeners and the Lees culminating in Patricia Lee's marriage to the Gardeners' son, Cecil. Cheltenham were one of the earliest manufactures to operate an owners' club and welcomed feedback from its members to help iron out any problems for future models. Ralph would occasionally road test Cheltenham prototypes as well as the occasional new release and his Standard Vanguard even featured in the pages of sales literature for the 1953 Cheltenham Eland.

In 1971, Ralph celebrated 50 years continuous membership with the Camping & Caravanning Club who duly presented him with a commemorative plaque. For his inspirational musings and outstanding contribution to caravan journalism, he also received an award from the Caravanners Writers Guild.

And then in 1999, Her Majesty The Queen invited Ralph to Buckingham Palace to receive an MBE for services to caravanning. Sadly, Muriel was not there to share the proud occasion having passed away six years earlier. After her death, Ralph curtailed the more ambitious expeditions abroad but continued to attend and support national and regional rallies.

When Ralph died in 2002, the Camping & Caravanning Club commissioned a seat for their Blackmore campsite in memory of the Lees and in recognition of Ralph's 81 years unbroken membership.

In their lifetime, Ralph and Muriel Lee clocked up over 500,000 miles with their various caravans, enough to take them twenty times around the world or, indeed, to the Moon!

ALSO AVAILABLE IN THIS SERIES

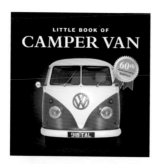

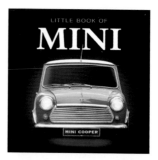

Enjoy the widest choice of superb sites

- **Access over 200 superb Club Sites**
- **Over 2,500 Certificated Locations - small five 'van sites**
- **Plus many other exclusive benefits and services**

Find out more

www.caravanclub.co.uk/littlebook

Freephone 0800 328 6635*

Opening hours 9.00am – 5.30pm Mondays to Fridays. Calls may be recorded

THE CARAVAN CLUB

The pictures in this book were provided courtesy of the following:

CARAVAN CLUB ARCHIVE
www.caravanclub.co.uk

NATIONAL MOTOR MUSEUM/MPL
nationalmotormuseum.org.uk

Design and artwork by Scott Giarnese

Published by G2 Entertainment Limited

Publishers Jules Gammond and Edward Adams

Written by Steve Lanham